Traveller's
ITALIAN

By bestselling author *Elisabeth Smith*

**Also available
in ebook**

Teach Yourself®

Traveller's
ITALIAN

Contents

Read this first   vi
How this book works   viii
Progress chart   x

Week 1   **Day-by-day guide**   1
In the aeroplane • *In aereo* • New words • Pronunciation •
Good news grammar • Let's speak Italian • Let's speak more
Italian • Let's speak Italian – fast and fluently • Learn by heart •
Test your progress

Week 2   **Day-by-day guide**   17
In Tuscany • *In Toscana* • New words • Good news grammar •
Let's speak Italian • Let's speak more Italian • Let's speak Italian –
fast and fluently • Learn by heart • Test your progress

Week 3   **Day-by-day guide**   31
We're going shopping • *Andiamo a fare spese* • New words •
Good news grammar • Learn by heart • Let's speak Italian •
Let's speak more Italian • Let's speak Italian – fast and fluently •
Spot the keys • Test your progress

Week 4   **Day-by-day guide**   45
Let's go and eat • *Andiamo a mangiare* • New words •
Good news grammar • Learn by heart • Say it simply •
Let's speak Italian • Let's speak more Italian • Let's speak Italian –
fast and fluently • Spot the keys • Test your progress

Week 5   **Day-by-day guide**   63
On the move • *In viaggio* • New words • Learn by heart •
Good news grammar • Let's speak Italian • Let's speak more
Italian • Let's speak Italian – fast and fluently • Spot the keys •
Test your progress

Week 6   **Day-by-day guide**   77
Day-by-day guide • In the airport • *In aeroporto* • New words •
Learn by heart • Good news grammar • Say it simply • Spot
the keys • Let's speak Italian • Let's speak more Italian • Let's
speak Italian – fast and fluently • Test your progress

Answers   92
Italian–English dictionary   98
English–Italian dictionary   105
Flash cards   112
Certificate   147

Read this first

If, like me, you usually skip introductions, don't. Read on. You need to know how **Traveller's Italian** works and why. You'll want to know how you are going to speak Italian in just six weeks.

When I decided to write this series I first called it *Barebones*, because that's what you want: no frills, no fuss, just the bare bones and go! So in **Traveller's Italian** you'll find:

- Only 379 words to say, well ... nearly everything.
- No tricky grammar – just some useful tips.
- No time wasters such as *the pen of my aunt...*
- No phrase book phrases for when you have a tooth extracted in Tuscany.
- No need to be perfect. Mistakes won't spoil your success.

I've put some 30 years of teaching experience into this course. I know how people learn. I also know how long they are motivated by a new project before the boredom sets in (a few weeks). And I am well aware how little time they can spare to study each day (about ½ hour). That's why you'll complete **Traveller's Italian** in six weeks and get away with 35 minutes a day.

Of course there is some learning to do, but I have tried to make it as much fun as possible. You'll meet Tom and Kate Walker on holiday in Italy. They do the kind of things you need to know about: shopping, eating out and getting about. They chat to the locals, ask a lot of questions and even understand the answers – most of the time! As you will note, Tom and Kate speak Italian all the time, even to each other. What paragons of virtue!

To get the most out of this course, there are only three things you really should do:

- Follow the **Day-by-day guide** as suggested. Please don't skip bits and short-change your success. Everything is there for a reason.
- If you are a complete beginner and have only bought the book, treat yourself to the recording as well. It will help you to speak faster and with confidence.
- Don't skip the next page (**How this book works**). It's essential for your success.

When you have filled in your **Certificate** at the end of the book and can speak **Traveller's Italian,** I would like to hear from you. Why not visit my website www.elisabeth-smith.co.uk, e-mail me at elisabeth.smith@hodder.co.uk, or write to me care of Hodder Education, 338 Euston Road, London, NW13BH?

And please join me on:

f Facebook at www.facebook.com/elisabethsmithlanguages

t Twitter at www.twitter.com/LanguagesESmith

Elizabeth Smith

How this book works

Traveller's Italian has been structured for your rapid success. This is how it works:

Day-by-day guide Stick to it. If you miss a day, add one.

Dialogues Follow Tom and Kate through Italy. The English of Weeks 1–3 is in 'Italian-speak' to get you tuned in. 'Italian-speak' is English imitating the expressions and word order of Italian: *We have a house big without telephone.* You'll soon get a feel for the language.

New words Don't fight them, don't skip them – learn them! The Flash cards and the recording will help you. Get your friends or family to test you. Or take the **flash cards** with you when you are out and about.

Good news grammar After you read it you can forget half and still succeed! That's why it's good news.

Flash words and flash sentences Read about these building blocks in the **Flash card** section. Then use them. They'll reduce learning time by 50%.

Learn by heart Obligatory! Memorizing puts you on the fast track to speaking in full sentences. When you know all six pieces you'll be able to speak in Italian for six minutes without drawing breath.

Let's speak Italian *You* will be doing the talking – in Italian.

Let's speak more Italian – fast and fluently Optional extras for more speaking practice without pausing and stumbling.

Spot the keys Listen to rapid Italian and make sense of it. Find the key words among a seemingly unintelligible string of sentences and get the gist of what's being said – an essential skill.

Say it simply Learn how to use simple Italian to say what you want to say. Don't be shy.

Test your progress Mark your own test and be amazed by the result.

Answers This is where you'll find the answers to the exercises.

🔊 This icon asks you to switch on the recording.

Pronunciation If you don't know about it and don't have the recording go straight to **Week 1 Pronunciation**. You need to know about pronunciation before you can start Week 1.

Progress chart Enter your score each week and monitor your progress. Are you going for *very good* or *outstanding?*

Dictionary Forgotten one of the new words? Look it up in the dictionary.

Certificate It's on the last page. In six weeks it will have your name on it.

Progress chart

At the end of each week record your test score on the progress chart below.

At the end of the course throw out your worst result – anybody can have a bad week – and add up your *five* best weekly scores. Divide the total by five to get your average score and overall course result. Write your result – *outstanding, excellent, very good* or *good* – on your **Certificate** at the end of the book.

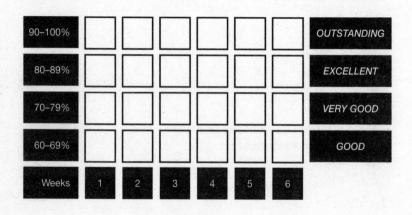

Total of five best weeks =

divided by five =

Your final result _____%

Week 1

Day-by-day guide

Invest 35 minutes a day – or a little longer if you can.

Day zero
- Read **Read this first!**
- Now read **How this book works**.

Day one
- Read **In the aeroplane**.
- Listen to/Read **In aereo**.
- Listen to/Read the **New words**, then learn some of them.

Day two
- Repeat **In aereo** and the **New words**.
- Listen to/Read **Pronunciation**.
- Learn more **New words**.
- Use the **Flash words** to help you.

Day three
- Learn all the **New words** until you know them well.
- Read and learn the **Good news grammar**.

Day four
- Cut out and learn the **Flash sentences**.
- Listen to/Read **Learn by heart**.

Day five
- Listen to/Read **Let's speak Italian**.
- Revise! Tomorrow you'll be testing your progress.

Day six
- Listen to/Read **Let's speak more Italian** (optional).
- Listen to/Read **Let's speak Italian – fast and fluently** (optional).
- Translate **Test your progress**.

Day seven – This is your day off.

In the aeroplane

Tom and Kate Walker are off to Italy. They board a plane to Florence via Milan and squeeze past a fellow passenger sitting in their row. Don't forget that the English of weeks 1–3 is in 'Italian-speak' to help you get used to the way the language works.

Tom   Excuse me, we have the seats 9a and 9b.

Gino   Yes, sure, one moment please.

Tom   Good day, we are Tom and Kate Walker.

Gino   Good morning, I am Pavarotti.

Tom   Luciano Pavarotti?

Gino   No, unfortunately. I am Gino Pavarotti.

Tom   We are going to Florence. Also you?

Gino   No, I am going to Milan. I am from Verona.

Tom   I was in Verona in April. Verona is very beautiful. I was in Verona for my company.

Gino   What do you do?

Tom   I work with the computers.

Gino   And you, Mrs Walker? What do you do? Where do you work?

Kate   I worked in a school for three years. Now I work at the Rover.

Gino   Are you from London?

Kate   No, we are from Manchester. We were one year in New York and two years in London. Now we are in Birmingham.

Gino   I worked for five years at the Fiat. Now I work at the Bank of Italy.

Tom   How is the work at the bank? Good?

Gino   The work is boring. I work too much but I need a lot of money. I have a big house, a Mercedes and four children. My wife is American. She has a girlfriend in Florida and telephones always. It costs a lot.

Kate   Now we are in holiday. Also you?

Gino   No, unfortunately. Not we are in holiday now. We are in holiday in August. We are going to Portofino but without children. We have a house there without telephone – and we go without mobile!

In aereo

🔊 CD1, tr 2

Tom and Kate Walker are on their way to Italy. They board a plane to Firenze via Milano and squeeze past a fellow passenger sitting in their row.

Tom   Scusi, abbiamo i posti nove a e nove b.

Gino   Sì, certo, un momento per favore.

Tom   Buongiorno, siamo Tom e Kate Walker.

Gino   Buongiorno, sono Pavarotti.

Tom   Luciano Pavarotti?

Gino   No, purtroppo. Sono Gino Pavarotti.

Tom   Andiamo a Firenze. Anche Lei?

Gino   No, vado a Milano. Sono di Verona.

Tom   Sono stato a Verona in aprile. Verona è molto bella. Sono stato a Verona per la mia ditta.

Gino   Che cosa fa?

Tom   Lavoro con i computer.

Gino   E Lei, Signora Walker? Cosa fa? Dove lavora?

Kate   Ho lavorato in una scuola per tre anni. Adesso lavoro alla Rover.

Gino   È di Londra?

Kate   No, siamo di Manchester. Siamo stati un anno a New York e due anni a Londra. Adesso siamo a Birmingham.

Gino   Io ho lavorato per cinque anni alla Fiat. Adesso lavoro alla Banca d'Italia.

Tom   Com'è il lavoro alla banca? Buono?

Gino   Il lavoro è noioso. Lavoro troppo ma ho bisogno di molti soldi. Ho una casa grande, una Mercedes e quattro bambini. Mia moglie è americana. Ha un'amica in Florida e telefona sempre. Costa molto.

Kate   Adesso siamo in vacanza. Anche Lei?

Gino   No, purtroppo. Non siamo in vacanza adesso. Siamo in vacanza in agosto. Andiamo a Portofino ma senza bambini. Abbiamo una casa là senza telefono – e andiamo senza telefonino!

New words

🔊 CD1, tr 3

Cover up the Italian words, then say them out loud.

in aereo in the aeroplane
scusi excuse me
abbiamo we have
il, la, i, le, l', gli the
posti seats, places
nove nine
a, b (*pronounced* **ah, bee**)
e and
sì yes
certo sure, certain
un momento a moment
per favore please
buongiorno good day, good morning, hello
il giorno the day
siamo we are
sono I am
no no
purtroppo unfortunately
andiamo we go, we are going
a to, at
anche also, too
Lei you
vado I go, am going
di from, of
sono stato/a I have been, I was
aprile April
è is he/she/it...? he/she/it is, you are
molto very, much, a lot
bello/a beautiful
per for
il mio, la mia my
ditta firm
che?, che cosa?, cosa? what?
fa you do/do you do?
lavoro I work, I am working

con with
Signora Mrs, woman
dove? where?
lavora you work, he/she/it works
ho; ho lavorato I have; I have worked, I worked
un, una, un' a
scuola school
tre three
anno, anni year, years
adesso now
al, alla at, at the
siamo stati we have been, we were
due two
io I (*only use to emphasize*)
cinque five
la Banca d'Italia The Bank of Italy
come how
com'è? (come è) how is...?
il lavoro the work
buono/a good
noioso/a boring
troppo too much
ma but
ho bisogno (di) I need
molti soldi a lot of money
casa house
grande big
quattro four
bambino/i child, children
moglie wife
americana American
ha he/she/it has, you have
amica girlfriend
telefona she/he telephones
sempre always

4

costa it costs	**là** there
in vacanza on holiday	**non** not
agosto August	**il telefono** the telephone
senza without	**il telefonino** the mobile phone

> **TOTAL NEW WORDS: 78**
> ...only 301 words to go!

Some easy extras

I mesi *(the months)*

gennaio	aprile	luglio	ottobre
febbraio	maggio	agosto	novembre
marzo	giugno	settembre	dicembre

I numeri *(the numbers)*

zero	uno	due	tre	quattro	cinque	sei	sette	otto	nove	dieci
0	1	2	3	4	5	6	7	8	9	10

More greetings

buona sera good evening **ciao** hello/goodbye
buona notte good night

Essential verbs for every day: 'to have' and 'to be'

In a couple of days you'll be reading about verbs in **Good news grammar**. Then on Day 3 spend ten minutes on these two verbs. I have framed them for you so you can't ignore them. But don't learn them today. Don't let's overdo it!

essere *to be*					
(io)	**sono**	*I am*	(noi)	**siamo**	*we are*
(Lei)	**è**	*you are*	(loro)	**sono**	*they are*
(lui)	**è**	*he/it is*			
(lei)	**è**	*she/it is*			

avere *to have*			
ho	*I have*	**abbiamo**	*we have*
ha	*you have*	**hanno**	*they have*
ha	*he/it has*		
ha	*she/it has*		

5

Pronunciation

◀ CD1, tr 4

The Italian language is beautiful, so drop all inhibitions and imagine that you're Italian. If Italian pronunciation is new to you, make sure you have a copy of the recording. But if you are good at languages, or want a refresher, here are the rules:

First the vowels

The English word in brackets gives you an example of the sound. Say the sound and the Italian examples out loud.

a	(*pasta*)	vado, fa, casa, grande
e	(*best*)	per, sempre, bella
i	(*field*)	il, sì, amica, arrivederci
o	(*not*)	no, non, sono, momento
u	(*June*)	scusi, un, una, purtroppo

When you come across two vowels next to each other, as in **euro**, **buono**, or **andiamo**, say each one separately: **e-u-ro**, **bu-o-no**, **andi-a-mo**.

Consonants

There are only two which could be confusing: **c** and **g**. Each of these comes in a 'hard' and 'soft' variety, so you need to know when it is a hard sound and when it is soft.

Soft c:	This sounds like the *ch* in *chocolate*.
(**c** before **e**)	Either of these two produces a 'soft' sound.
(**c** before **i**)	***Examples:*** **certo, cinque**
Note: **cia, cio**	Soft **c**, but the **i** is not pronounced. **C(i)ao!**
	Luc(i)ano, dic(i)otto
Hard c:	This sounds like the *c* in *coffee*.
c, ch	Either of these two produce the 'hard' sound.
	Examples: **casa, cosa, scusi, che, chilo** *(kilo)*, **cliente, credo**

Soft g:	This sounds like the *j* in *jet*.
(**g** before **e**)	Either of these two produces a 'soft' sound.
(**g** before **i**)	***Examples:* Gino, Genova, viaggi**
gia, gio, giu	Soft **g**, but the **i** is not pronounced.
	***Examples:* g(i)allo** (*yellow*)**, g(i)orno, G(i)useppe**
Hard g:	This sounds like the *g* in *good*.
g, gh	Either of these two produces a 'hard' sound.
	***Examples:* golf, grande, spaghetti, Inghilterra** (*England*)

Special sounds

Soft sc:	This sounds like the *sh* in *ship*.
(**sc** before **e**)	Either of these two produces a 'soft' sound.
(**sc** before **i**)	***Examples:* scena** (*scene*)**, sci** (*ski*)
h	This is always silent: **ho, ha:** say *o* and *a*!
gn	This sounds like the *ny* in *canyon*.
	***Examples:* bisogno** (say: '**bisonyo**')
gl	This sounds like the '*lyer*' sound in the word *million*: **moglie** (say '**mol-ye**'), **gli** (say '**lyee**').
s	(between vowels) This sounds like the *z* in *zombie*.
	***Examples:* cosa, casa**
	But at the beginning of a word, or before a consonant, it sounds like the *s* in *sun*: **sì, scuola, costa, essere.**
z	This sounds like the **z** in *zombie* – but pretend there is a *t* in front of the **z** (say: '**tzombie**').
	***Examples:* agenzia, vacanze**
Doubles:	Try to stretch these. Pretend there are four of them!
gg, ll, nn, etc.	***Examples:* bello, anno, mamma**

Roll your 'r's!

Note that the Italian **r** always has a clear rolled sound, unlike English.

Examples: **favore, troppo, signora, Inghilterra**

Which syllable to stress

You usually stress the last-but-one part of the word:

scu-si, ab-bi-a-mo, pos-ti, mo-men-to

But as always there are exceptions – sorry!

te-le-fo-na, cre-di-to

There is a written accent when the stress falls on the last vowel:

caffè *(coffee)*, **perché** *(because)*, **lunedì** *(Monday)*

and to differentiate between words spelt the same way.

Good news grammar

🔊 CD1, tr 5

This is the **Good news** part of each week. Remember I promised: No confusing grammar!

I simply explain the differences between English and Italian. This will help you to speak Italian easily.

1 Names of things – nouns

There are two kinds of nouns in Italian: masculine and feminine.

You can tell which is which by the word **il** or **la** (*the*), or **un** or **una** (*a* or *one*) in front of the word. You can also tell by the ending of the noun.

Most masculine nouns end in **-o**: **il lavoro, il telefono, un momento**.

Most feminine nouns end in **-a**: **la ditta, una casa**.

The adjective describing the noun also ends in **-o** or **-a**. So *the good work* or *house* becomes: **il lavoro buono** or **una casa buona**.

When you talk about more than one thing (plural) the **il** and **la** change into **i** and **le**.

And to complete the jigsaw, all words ending in **-o** and **-a** end in **-i** and **-e** in the plural.

> *i* **posti buoni** *the good seats*
> *le* **case belle** *the beautiful houses*

This may sound complicated, but it is really easy, and you'll learn it without even noticing. If you get muddled and say **il casa bello** or **le vacanze buoni**, Italians will still understand you perfectly.

Some nouns end in **-e,** so you can't tell what they are. In the **New words** they have **il** or **la** in front of them so you'll know.

The plural of **-e** is **-i**: **cane** → **cani** (*dog* → *dogs*).

2 Doing things – verbs

Unlike the English, the Italians do not use *I*, *you*, *he*, *she*, *it*, *we*, or *they* to identify who is doing something unless they wish to clarify or stress it. So the only way you can tell who is doing something is by the verb itself.

Each person has his or her own verb form or verb ending, but sometimes a verb or an ending is shared. This could lead to some confusion, but amazingly it usually works out all right.

There are a few verbs which you'll use every day. I have put the first two in a box in the **New words** section. Learn them now, it won't take long.

3 Asking questions

This is very easy. In Italian there is no difference between *Rome is beautiful* (**Roma è bella**) and *Is Rome beautiful?* (**Roma è bella?**).

Here's another example: *It costs a lot.* (**Costa molto.**) *Does it cost a lot?* (**Costa molto?**)

Just use your voice to turn a statement into a question.

Let's speak Italian

🔊 CD1, tr 6

Here are ten English sentences. Read each sentence and say it in Italian out loud. You can check your answers on the recording if you have it.

1 Are you from London?
2 Yes, I am from London.
3 I am on holiday in August.
4 We are going to Como.
5 I was in Milan for my firm.
6 Do you have a Ferrari?
7 No, unfortunately.
8 We have a house in Rome.
9 How is the job with Fiat, good?
10 No, it is boring, but I need a lot of money.

Well, how many did you get right? If you are not happy, do it again.

Here are some questions in Italian. Answer these in Italian. Start every answer with **Sì** and talk about yourself.

11 È di Manchester?
12 Ha una casa a Londra?
13 Andiamo a Firenze. Anche Lei?
14 Lavora in una ditta a Torino?
15 Il lavoro è buono?

Now tell someone in Italian…

16 …that you have two children.
17 …that you have been in Torino.
18 …that you have a Fiat Punto.
19 …that you need a girlfriend.
20 …that Birmingham is boring in November.

Answers

1 È di Londra?
2 Sì, sono di Londra.
3 Sono in vacanza in agosto.
4 Andiamo a Como.
5 Sono stato (or stata) a Milano per la mia ditta.
6 Ha una Ferrari?
7 No, purtroppo.
8 Abbiamo una casa a Roma.
9 Com'è il lavoro alla Fiat, buono?
10 No, è noioso, ma ho bisogno di molti soldi.
11 Sì, sono di Manchester.
12 Sì, ho una casa a Londra.
13 Sì, vado a Firenze.
14 Sì, lavoro in una ditta a Torino.
15 Sì, il lavoro è buono.
16 Ho due bambini.
17 Sono stato/stata a Torino.
18 Ho una Fiat Punto.
19 Ho bisogno di un'amica.
20 Birmingham è noiosa in novembre.

Well, what was your score? If you got 15 out of 20 or more you have done very well.

Let's speak more Italian

🔊 CD1, tr 7

Here are some optional exercises. They may stretch the 35 minutes a day by 15 minutes. But the extra practice will be worth it.

And always remember: near enough is good enough!

In your own words

This exercise will teach you to express yourself freely. Use only the words you have learned so far.

Tell me in your own words that...

Example   *you are Peter Smith*
Sono Peter Smith.

1 you originate from Manchester
2 you have an American friend
3 you are a workaholic...
4 ...but you don't have a lot of cash
5 you have two children
6 the children are six and eight (have six and eight years)
7 unfortunately you work with PCs; the work is not interesting
8 your wife works in a bank
9 you own a property in Portofino
10 your children are in Birmingham

Answers

1 **Sono di Manchester.**
2 **Ho un amico americano/un'amica americana.**
3 **Lavoro molto...**
4 **...ma non ho molti soldi.**
5 **Ho due bambini.**
6 **I bambini hanno sei e otto anni.**
7 **Purtroppo lavoro con i computer; il lavoro non è interessante.**
8 **Mia moglie lavora in una banca.**
9 **Ho una casa a Portofino.**
10 **I miei bambini sono a Birmingham.**

13

Let's speak more Italian

Let's speak Italian – fast and fluently

🔊 CD1, tr 8

No more stuttering and stumbling. Get out the stopwatch and time yourself with this fluency practice.

Translate each section and check if it is correct, then cover up the answers and say the three or four sentences as quickly as you can. Try to say each paragraph in less than 20 seconds. Some of the English is in 'Italian-speak' to help you.

Good evening. I am going to Milan. You, too?
No, I work in Verona – for a bank. But I am going to Turin.
I am on holiday – without computer.

Buonasera. Vado a Milano. Anche Lei?
No, io lavoro a Verona – per una banca. Ma vado a Torino.
Sono in vacanza – senza computer.

How is Portofino? Is it (feminine) big?
No, it is not big, but it is interesting.
It is very beautiful and very expensive.
A house in Portofino, it costs a lot of money.

Com'è Portofino? È grande?
No, non è grande, ma è interessante.
È molto bella e molto cara.
Una casa a Portofino costa molto.

I have a girlfriend, Gina.
She has a house in Como.
Oh, excuse me. One moment, please, it is Gina.
She is always on the phone. Bye!

Ho un'amica, Gina.
Ha una casa a Como.
Oh, scusi. Un momento, per favore, è Gina.
È sempre al telefono. Arrivederci!

Now say all the sentences in Italian without stopping and starting.

Learn by heart

🔊 CD1, tr 9

Don't be tempted to skip this exercise because it reminds you of school. If you want to speak, not stumble, saying a few lines by heart does the trick.

Learn **Buongiorno** by heart after you have filled in the gaps with your personal, or any other information. Say **Buongiorno** out loud and fairly fast. Can you beat 40 seconds?

Buongiorno!

Buongiorno, sono ....(name).

Sono di ....(place).

Sono stato/a* a ....(place) in........................(month).

Ho lavorato alla .... (firm) per due anni.

Adesso lavoro alla ....(firm).

Ho una casa grande a ....(place) e costa molto.

In agosto andiamo a ....(place).

Com'è Firenze in aprile? bella?

*stato *if you are male,* stata *if you are female*

Test your progress

This is your only written exercise. You'll be amazed how easy it is!
Translate the 20 sentences without looking at the previous pages.

1 Good morning, we are Helen and Jane.
2 I am from Rome, you too?
3 Where do you work now?
4 I was in Milan in October.
5 My girlfriend is in Italy for one year.
6 We always go to Pisa in June.
7 I worked at Fiat in May.
8 What do you do in London?
9 I work in a school but without money.
10 The big house in Bologna is for the children.
11 One moment please, where is Luigi?
12 Does the house have a (the) telephone? No, unfortunately.
13 Does the Ferrari cost a lot? Yes, sure, it costs too much.
14 How is the work in Italy, good?
15 Mario has a friend in an American firm.
16 We were in Como for three days.
17 We have (the) good seats in aeroplane.
18 I always have (the) boring holidays.
19 I need a beautiful wife, a Lamborghini and a lot of money...
20 He telephones now with a firm in London.

When you have finished, look up the answers in the **Answers** section
and mark your work. Then enter your result on the **Progress chart**
at the front of the book. If your score is higher than 80% you'll have
done very well indeed!

Week 2
Day-by-day guide

35 minutes a day – but a little extra will step up your progress!

Day one
- Read **In Tuscany**.
- Listen to/Read **In Toscana**.
- Listen to/Read the **New words**. Learn 20 easy ones.

Day two
- Repeat **In Toscana** and the **New words**.
- Go over **Pronunciation**, if you need to.
- Learn the harder **New words**.
- Use the **Flash words** to help you.

Day three
- Learn all the **New words** until you know them well.
- Read and learn the **Good news grammar**.

Day four
- Cut out and learn the ten **Flash sentences**.
- Have a first go at **Let's speak Italian**.

Day five
- Listen to/Read **Let's speak Italian**.
- Listen to/Read **Learn by heart**.

Day six
- Listen to/Read **Let's speak more Italian** (optional).
- Listen to/Read **Let's speak Italian – fast and fluently** (optional).
- Go over **Non ho molti soldi...**
- Translate **Test your progress**.

Day seven – is a study-free day!

In Tuscany

Tom and Kate hire a car and drive through Tuscany. They book into a hotel and then look for somewhere to have a drink.

Kate   Good day. Do you have a room double for one night and not too expensive?

Hotelier   Yes, we have a room a little small with bath and shower. But the shower is broken. Perhaps my husband it can repair.

Tom   Where is the room?

Hotelier   It is here on the left. Is it enough big?

Tom   It is a little small but not it is bad. How much costs it?

Hotelier   Only €40 euros for two, but no cards of credit! The breakfast is from eight to nine and half.

Tom   All right, it we take. But can we make breakfast at eight less a quarter? Tomorrow at eight and a quarter we would like to go to Portofino.

Kate   And excuse me, where can we drink something?
There is a bar here?

Hotelier   There are two bars at five minutes from here. Not it is difficult. 30 metres on the right and then always straight on.

(In the bar...)

Waiter   What would you like?

Kate   We would like a coffee and a tea with milk.

Waiter   Would you like also something to eat?

Tom   What is there?

Waiter   We have cake of apples or rolls.

Kate   Two rolls with ham, please.

Tom   The ham not is good.

Kate   The mine is very good.

Tom   The table is too small.

Kate   But the toilets are big and very clean.

Tom   The tea is cold.

Kate   But the waiter is very handsome.

Tom   Waiter, the bill please!

Waiter   €9.10, please.

In Toscana

🔊 CD1, tr 10

Tom and Kate hire a car and drive through toscana. They book into a hotel and then look for somewhere to have a drink.

Kate   Buongiorno. Ha una camera doppia per una notte e non troppo cara?

Hotelier Sì, abbiamo una camera un po' piccola con bagno e doccia. Però la doccia è rotta. Forse mio marito la può riparare.

Tom   Dov'è la camera?

Hotelier È qui a sinistra. È abbastanza grande?

Tom   È un po' piccola ma non è male. Quanto costa?

Hotelier Solo quaranta euro per due, però niente carte di credito! La prima colazione è dalle otto alle nove e mezza.

Tom   Va bene, la prendiamo. Però possiamo fare colazione alle otto meno un quarto? Domani alle otto e un quarto vorremmo andare a Portofino.

Kate   E scusi, dove possiamo bere qualcosa? C'è un bar qui?

Hotelier Ci sono due bar a cinque minuti da qui. Non è difficile. Trenta metri a destra e poi sempre diritto.

(Nel bar...)

Waiter   Cosa desiderano?

Kate   Vorremmo un caffè e un tè con latte.

Waiter   Desiderano anche qualcosa da mangiare?

Tom   Che cosa c'è?

Waiter   Abbiamo della torta di mele o dei panini.

Kate   Due panini con prosciutto, per favore.

Tom   Il prosciutto non è buono.

Kate   Il mio è molto buono.

Tom   La tavola è troppo piccola.

Kate   Però i servizi sono grandi e molto puliti.

Tom   Il tè è freddo.

Kate   Ma il cameriere è molto bello.

Tom   Cameriere, il conto per favore!

Waiter   Nove euro e dieci, per favore.

New words

🔊 CD1, tr 11

Learning words the traditional way can be boring. If you enjoyed the Flash cards why not make your own for the rest of the words. Always say the words out loud.

camera room
doppio/a double
la notte the night
caro/a expensive, dear
un po', un pochino a little, a very little
piccolo/a small
bagno bath
però but
doccia shower
rotto/a broken
forse perhaps
marito husband
lo, la (by itself) it, him, her, you
può he/she/it/you can
riparare to repair
qui here
a sinistra on the left
abbastanza enough
male bad
quanto/a? how much...?
solo only
niente no, nothing, not anything
carta di credito credit card
la prima colazione the breakfast
da – a from – to/until
dalle otto... from eight o'clock lit. from the eight (hours)
mezzo, mezza half
va bene all right, OK
prendiamo we'll take
prendere to take
possiamo we can

fare colazione to have breakfast
meno less/before (with time)
un quarto a quarter
domani tomorrow
vorremmo we would like
andare to go
bere to drink
qualcosa something
c'è there is
ci sono there are
minuto, minuti minute, minutes
difficile difficult
a destra on the right
poi then
diritto straight on
nel bar in the bar
il cameriere the waiter
cosa desiderano? what would you like?
il caffè the coffee
il tè the tea
il latte the milk
da mangiare (something to) eat
torta di mele apple cake (cake of apples)
o or
panino, panini roll, rolls
prosciutto ham
tavola table
i servizi the toilets
pulito/a clean
freddo/a cold
conto bill

> **TOTAL NEW WORDS: 62**
> **...only 239 to go!**

Some useful extras

I numeri *(numbers)*

11 **undici**	*19* **diciannove**	*60* **sessanta**
12 **dodici**	*20* **venti**	*70* **settanta**
13 **tredici**	*21* **ventuno**	*80* **ottanta**
14 **quattordici**	*22* **ventidue**	*90* **novanta**
15 **quindici**	*23* **ventitré**	*100* **cento**
16 **sedici**	*30* **trenta**	*200* **duecento**
17 **diciassette**	*40* **quaranta**	*1.000* **mille**
18 **diciotto**	*50* **cinquanta**	

Il tempo *(time)*

a che ora?	*at what time?*	**un'ora**	*an hour*
alle cinque	*at five o'clock*	**un giorno**	*a day*
è l'una	*it is one o'clock*	**una settimana**	*a week*
sono le due	*it is two o'clock*	**un mese**	*a month*
un minuto	*a minute*	**un anno**	*a year*

half past = and half   **e mezzo**
quarter past = and a quarter   **e un quarto**
quarter to = less a quarter   **meno un quarto**

Good news grammar

🔊 CD1, tr 12

1 I, you, he, she, we, they

In Italian these are: **io**, **Lei** or **tu**, **lui**, **lei**, **noi**, **loro**. But, as you know, they are only used for emphasis: *I do this, you did that*. **Lei** (*you*), as opposed to **lei** (*she*), takes a capital **L**. **Lei** is the formal and polite way of saying *you*. When you are in Italy and speaking Fast-track Italian use **Lei**. **Tu** (and its plural **voi**) is for family and friends, and requires a great deal more extra grammar. Next year!

2 Saying *non* ('not')

Did you notice what happened to *not* when Signor Pavarotti said:

> **Non abbiamo le vacanze adesso.**
> *Not we have the holidays now.*

The *not* moved in front of the verb. It does this all the time:

> **Il lavoro è buono. Il lavoro non è buono.**
> *The work not is good.*

3 Verbs – again

This week's good news: two more everyday verbs – *can* and *go* – put into 'boxes' for easy learning. You'll need only a few minutes this time, because there is a bit of a pattern to each verb:

- *I* usually ends in **-o**: **sono, ho, vado, lavoro.**
- *you*, *he*, *she* and *it* end in **-e** or **-a**: **è, ha, va, lavora**, but **può** (*sorry*)
- *we* usually ends in **-iamo**: **andiamo, abbiamo, possiamo, prendiamo**
- *they* usually ends in **-ono** or **-an(n)o**: **sono, possono, hanno, vanno**

Simple, isn't it?

Now learn **andare** and **potere**. Spend five minutes on each.

andare	*to go*
vado	*I go*
va	*you go, he, she, it goes*
andiamo	*we go*
vanno	*they go*

potere	can
posso	I can
può	you can, he, she, it can
possiamo	we can
possono	they can

More good news: there's a complete summary of verbs in **Week 6 Good news grammar** – if you get confused. Why don't you have a look? You'll know most of these in four weeks' time.

4 *C'è/ci sono*: there is – is there?/there are – are there?

You will use this a lot, especially when asking questions.

> *C'è* un bar qui. Che cosa *c'è*? *Ci sono* servizi?
> *C'è* un cameriere molto bello?... Sì, sì...!

5 No collisions!

When two, usually identical, vowels meet, like **a + a** or **e + e**, one is dropped:

> **un'amica** *(not* **una amica***)*, **dov'è** *(not* **dove è***)*, **c'è** *(not* **ce è***)*.

6 Della, dei

This is just a way of saying **some** *cake* or **some** *rolls*. Nothing too serious.

Let's speak Italian

◀) CD1, tr 13

Now let's practise what you have learned. Here are ten English sentences for you to say in Italian out loud. Check your answers. If you didn't get them all right, do the exercise again.

1 We would like a room.
2 At what time is there breakfast?
3 The telephone is broken.
4 How much is (costs) the room?
5 Where is the bar, on the right or on the left?
6 Is there something to eat?
7 All right, we take it.
8 Can we go to Florence?
9 We would like to go at half past two.
10 Excuse me, the bill please.

Now answer in Italian. Use **Sì** and speak about yourself.

11 Va alle otto e mezza?
12 Può mangiare un panino?
13 Ha una carta di credito?

Now answer with **No** and speak for yourself and a friend:

14 Ha una tavola per quattro?
15 Può riparare la Rover?
16 Va a Roma domani?

And now answer freely. Your answers may differ from mine but be correct.

17 Dov'è la pensione Rossi?
18 Com'è la camera?
19 Dove c'è un bar qui?
20 A che ora va a Milano Gina?

Answers

1 Vorremmo una camera.
2 A che ora c'è la prima colazione?
3 Il telefono è rotto.
4 Quanto costa la camera?
5 Dov'è il bar, a destra o a sinistra?
6 C'è qualcosa da mangiare?
7 Va bene, lo (or la) prendiamo.
8 Possiamo andare a Firenze?
9 Vorremmo andare alle due e mezza.
10 Scusi, il conto per favore.
11 Sì, vado alle otto e mezza.
12 Sì, posso mangiare un panino.
13 Sì, ho una carta di credito.
14 No, non abbiamo una tavola per quattro.
15 No, non possiamo riparare la Rover (or ripararla).
16 No, domani non andiamo a Roma.
17 La pensione Rossi è in Toscana.
18 La camera è un po' piccola ma non è male.
19 C'è un bar a dieci minuti da qui, a sinistra e poi sempre diritto.
20 (Gina) Va a Milano alle otto.

Did you get more than half right the first time? If you did, give yourself a pat on the back.

Let's speak more Italian

◀))) CD1, tr 14

Here are the two optional exercises. Remember, they may stretch the 35 minutes a day by 15 minutes. But the extra practice will be worth it.

In your own words

This exercise will teach you to express yourself freely.

Use only the words you have learned so far, and where possible answer using the verb form for we.

Ask me in your own words...

1 if an en suite double room is available
2 what the price of the room is for one night
3 where you can have (take) a coffee

Tell me...

4 that there is a café at 20 minutes from here; you go straight ahead
5 you would like (the) breakfast at 7.30
6 you are thinking of going to Portofino tomorrow
7 you would like two coffees and some cake of apples
8 what you don't like about the café (the table is too small and the cake isn't good)
9 what Kate likes about the café (the toilets are clean and the waiter is very handsome)
10 that the bill is €9.60

Answers

1 **Ha una camera doppia con bagno o doccia?**
2 **Quanto costa per una notte?**
3 **Dove possiamo prendere un caffè?**
4 **C'è un bar a venti minuti da qui. Sempre diritto.**
5 **Vorremmo la prima colazione alle sette e mezza.**
6 **Vorremmo andare a Portofino domani.**
7 **Vorremmo due caffè e della torta di mele.**
8 **La tavola è troppo piccola e la torta non è buona.**
9 **I servizi sono puliti, e il cameriere è molto bello.**
10 **Il conto è nove euro e sessanta.**

Let's speak Italian – fast and fluently

🔊 CD1, tr 15

No more stuttering and stumbling. Get out the stopwatch and time yourself with this fluency practice.

Translate each section and check if it is correct, then cover up the answers and say the three or four sentences fast.

Try to say each paragraph in less than 20 seconds.

Some of the English is in 'Italian-speak' to help you.

Good evening, do you have a room with bath?
80 euros is a little expensive.
We would like a room with shower.
How much is the breakfast? We can make breakfast at 7 o'clock?

Buonasera, ha una camera con bagno?
Ottanta euro è un po' cara.
Vorremmo una camera con doccia.
Quanto costa la prima colazione? Possiamo fare colazione alle sette?

Where is my house? Straight ahead, then to the right.
But we are going tomorrow to Pisa.
We would like to go at nine hours and half.

Dov'è la mia casa? Sempre diritto, poi a destra.
Ma domani andiamo a Pisa.
Vorremmo andare alle nove e mezza.

The bar here is very small and very expensive.
But the coffee is good, and the rolls with ham are excellent.
The bill, please. How much? €38 for two coffees and two rolls?
We do not have enough money!

Il bar qui è molto piccolo e molto caro.
Ma il caffè è buono, e i panini con prosciutto sono molto buoni.
Il conto, per favore. Quanto? Trentotto euro per due caffè e due panini?
Non abbiamo abbastanza soldi!

Now say all the sentences in Italian without stopping and starting.

Try to do it in under one minute.

But if you are not happy with your result – just try once more.

Learn by heart

Learn the seven lines **Non ho molti soldi però...** by heart. Try to say them with a bit of 'drama' in 45–60 seconds. Choose one of these to fill the gap: **mio marito, mia moglie, il mio amico, la mia amica**.

Non ho molti soldi però...

Non ho molti soldi però vorrei* andare in Italia con ...

Vorremmo andare a Portofino con la Rover.

È molto bello in aprile.

La pensione Rossi non è molto cara.

Quanto costa? Solo quaranta euro a notte.

Lo posso fare?

No. C'è sempre troppo lavoro nella mia ditta, e – la Rover è rotta!

*vorrei: *I would like to*

Test your progress

Translate the following sentences in writing. What do you remember without checking back?

1 Where is there a telephone?
2 Excuse me, we only have a (the) credit card.
3 Can we eat at seven tomorrow?
4 Do you have a big enough table? We are (in) five.
5 The small rooms do not have a (the) bath.
6 We would like to eat ham and melon (**melone**).
7 We can go from six to quarter to seven.
8 Where can we drink something?
9 We have been in the (**al**) bar from nine to half past ten.
10 All right, we take the Fiat for a day.
11 How much does the breakfast cost? Only €5.
12 Let's go and (to) repair the computer. It is broken.
13 How is the milk? Can the child drink it?
14 Where are the toilets, on the right or on the left?
15 Can I go to Hollywood – without my husband?
16 A coffee, please – nothing for you?
17 Where is (the) Signora Rossi? Perhaps in the (**nel**) bar?
18 €3.10 for a cold tea – it is a little expensive!
19 I have been in Tuscany in February. It is not bad.
20 There are 300 bars here, one at a hundred metres from here.

Check your answers. The **Progress chart** awaits your score!

Week 3

Day-by-day guide

Study for 35 minutes a day – but there are no penalties for doing more!

Day one
- Read **We're going shopping**.
- Listen to/Read **Andiamo a fare spese**.
- Read the **New words**, then learn some of them.

Day two
- Repeat **Andiamo a fare spese** and the **New words**.
- Learn all the **New words**. Use the **Flash cards**.

Day three
- Test yourself on all the **New words** – rather boring, but you are over halfway already.
- Learn the **Good news grammar**.

Day four
- Cut out and learn the **Flash sentences**.
- Listen to/Read **Learn by heart**.

Day five
- Listen to/Read **Let's speak Italian**.
- Listen to/Read **Spot the keys**.

Day six
- Listen to/Read **Let's speak more Italian** (optional).
- Listen to/Read **Let's speak Italian – fast and fluently** (optional).
- Have a quick look at the **New words** from Weeks 1–3. You now know 218 words ... well, more or less.
- Translate **Test your progress**.

Day seven – This is your day off!

We're going shopping

Next stop Portofino and a week in a holiday apartment. Kate plans to do some shopping but Tom is less keen.

Kate Today we must do the shopping. Let's go into the centre with the bus.

Tom But there is bad weather, it makes cold and there is a lot of sport in television... the golf at two and half...

Kate I am sorry, but we must first go to the cashpoint machine and to the post office or to the tobacconist for the stamps... then into chemist's and into dry cleaner's.

Tom In that case no golf... perhaps the football at four and a quarter... is it all?

Kate No, we have to go in a big store to buy a suitcase new. Then I have to go to the supermarket and to the hairdresser's. And afterwards I would like to buy some shoes.

Tom Bother...! Until when are open the shops?

Kate Until seven and half, I believe.

Tom Therefore no football... perhaps the tennis at eight.

(Later...)

Kate Hello Tom, here is the shopping: 200 grams of ham, a piece of cheese, half a kilo of apples, two kilos of potatoes, a mozzarella, sugar, bread, butter, some eggs, six beers and a bottle of wine. I have bought too much.

Tom It doesn't matter. Yesterday not we have eaten much. And what is there in the bag big? Something for me?

Kate Well... near to the UPIM there was a shop small and I have seen some shoes which were of my size. Not are they beautiful? White and blue. The sales assistant was very nice and handsome like Tom Cruise.

Tom Who is Tom Cruise? And how much cost the shoes?

Kate They were a very little expensive... but they cost the same in England...€100.

Tom What? My wife is crazy!

Kate But this T-shirt for the golf was very cheap. Size 42, only €10. Here is a newspaper English... and now not is there the tennis in television?

Andiamo a fare spese

🔊 CD1, tr 17

Next stop Portofino and a week in holiday apartment. Kate plans to do some shopping but Tom is less keen.

Kate   Oggi dobbiamo fare spese. Andiamo in centro con l'autobus.

Tom   Ma c'è brutto tempo, fa freddo e c'è molto sport in televisione… il golf alle due e mezza…

Kate   Mi dispiace ma dobbiamo prima passare al Bancomat e alla posta o dal tabaccaio per i francobolli… poi in farmacia e in tintoria.

Tom   Dunque niente golf… forse il calcio alle quattro e un quarto… è tutto?

Kate   No, dobbiamo andare in un grande magazzino per comprare una valigia nuova. Poi devo passare al supermercato e dal parrucchiere. E dopo vorrei comprare delle scarpe.

Tom   Uffa…! Fino a quando sono aperti i negozi?

Kate   Fino alle sette e mezza, credo.

Tom   Dunque niente calcio… forse il tennis alle otto.

(Più tardi…)

Kate   Ciao, Tom, ecco la spesa: 200 grammi di prosciutto, un pezzo di formaggio, mezzo chilo di mele, due chili di patate, una mozzarella, zucchero, pane, burro, qualche uovo, sei birre e una bottiglia di vino. Ho comprato troppo.

Tom   Non importa. Ieri non abbiamo mangiato molto. E cosa c'è nella borsa grande? Qualcosa per me?

Kate   Beh… Vicino alla UPIM c'era un negozio piccolo e ho visto delle scarpe che erano del mio numero. Non sono belle? Bianche e blu. Il commesso era molto simpatico e bello come Tom Cruise.

Tom   Chi è Tom Cruise? E quanto costano le scarpe?

Kate   Erano un pochino care… ma costano lo stesso in Inghilterra… cento euro.

Tom   Cosa? Mia moglie è pazza!

Kate   Però questa T-shirt per il golf era molto conveniente. Taglia 42, solo dieci euro. Ecco un giornale inglese… e adesso non c'è il tennis in televisione?

New words

🔊 CD1, tr 18

Learn the **New words** in half the time using the flash cards.
There are 22 to start you off.

fare spese to do (the) shopping
oggi today
dobbiamo we must
centro centre
autobus bus
brutto bad, ugly
tempo weather (*also* time)
fa freddo it is cold (*used with weather*)
la televisione the TV
mi dispiace I am sorry
prima first
passare a/da pass, call on, go to
da from, by, *also:* at someone's house
il Bancomat a cashpoint machine
posta post office
il tabaccaio the tobacconist's (*sells stamps*)
francobolli stamps
farmacia chemist's, pharmacy
tintoria dry cleaner's
dunque therefore, in that case
calico football
tutto all
grande magazzino department store
comprare to buy

valigia suitcase
nuovo/a new
supermercato supermarket
il parrucchiere the hairdresser's
dopo after, afterwards
vorrei I would like
negozio, negozi shop, shops
le scarpe the shoes
uffa! something you say when you are fed up
fino a until
quando when
aperto open
credo I think, believe
più tardi later
ecco here, here is/here are
la spesa the shopping
grammi grams
pezzo piece
formaggio cheese
chilo kilo
patate potatoes
zucchero sugar
il pane bread
burro butter
qualche some
uovo, uova egg, eggs
birra, birre beer, beers
bottiglia bottle

vino wine
ho comprato I bought, have bought
non importa no problem, it doesn't matter
ieri yesterday
abbiamo mangiato we ate, have eaten
borsa bag
me, mi me
beh… well…
vicino, vicino a near, near to
la UPIM *well-known Italian chain store*
era/erano was/were

ho visto I have seen
bianco white
blu blue
commesso/a sales assistant
simpatico/a nice
chi who
costano they cost
lo stesso the same
Inghilterra England
pazzo/a crazy
questo/a this
conveniente cheap
taglia size
il giornale the newspaper
inglese English

> TOTAL NEW WORDS: 78…
> only 161 words to go!

Some easy extras: *i colori* (colours)

bianco *white*	**nero** *black*	**rosso** *red*	**blu** *blue*
verde *green*	**giallo** *yellow*	**marrone** *brown*	**grigio** *grey*
arancione *orange*	**rosa** *pink*		

Good news grammar

◀)) CD1, tr 19

1 Doing more things with verbs: the past

Imagine you were getting married today. You would say *I do*. If it happened yesterday, you would say *I did* or *I have done it*. To talk about something that happened before or in the past, in Italian you use *have* – which you know already – plus a slightly changed main verb.

So, **mangiare** becomes **mangiato** and **comprare** becomes **comprato**.

I bought, or *I have bought*	**ho comprato**
you bought, or *you have bought*	
he/she/it bought, or *has bought*	**ha comprato**
we bought, or *we have bought*	**abbiamo comprato**
they bought, or *they have bought*	**hanno comprato**

And how about **mangiare**? How would you say *We ate!*? **Abbiamo mangiato!** What about **riparare**? How would you ask *Have you repaired?* **Ha riparato? Sì!**

Unfortunately, you do not use *have* with all verbs. Here are a couple of 'rebels'.

essere	*to be*	**sono stato/a**	*I was, I have been*
andare	*to go*	**sono andato/a**	*I went, I have gone*

As you can see, **andare** (*go*) and **essere** (*be*) behave very strangely.

Instead of *I **have*** you say *I **am** gone* and *I **am** been*.

Are you gone to Milano?	**È andato a Milano?**
No, I am not gone...	**No, non sono andato.**

No need to panic. By the end of Week 6 these two will be good friends.

2 Joining little words: turning two into one

Italians love their language to be smooth. Little pairs like *to–the*, *of–the* or *from–the* sound too 'staccato' to them so they 'melt' the two words into one. Here are six to give you a feel for them:

a + il = al	**da + il = dal**	**su + la = sulla**
di + la = della	**in + il = nel**	**con + il = col**

And if you don't 'melt'? No problem. Everyone will understand you.

3 *Passare da/a/in*

They all mean *to go to...*

> **passo *dal* tabaccaio** (*I am going to the tabbacconist's*)
> **passo *al* Bancomat** (*I am going to the cashpoint machine*)
> **passo *in* farmacia** (*I am going to the pharmacy*)

Don't worry if you use the wrong one – you will still be understood, and nobody will laugh.

4 *Il mio, la mia, il suo, la sua*

When Italians say *my*, *your*, *his*, or *her* they always add *the*.

il mio cane	*my dog*
la sua ditta	*his/her company*

Sounds very grand, doesn't it?

Funnily enough, when you talk about your partner you simply say: **mio marito** or **mia moglie**. By the way, if you forget, it doesn't matter!

Learn by heart

◀) CD1, tr 20

Say this dialogue in under one minute and with a lot of expression!

Dobbiamo fare spese... Uffa!

Tom   Oggi fa freddo. C'è il calcio in televisione.

Kate   Mi dispiace ma dobbiamo fare spese. Non abbiamo niente da mangiare. Dobbiamo prima passare al Bancomat e dopo al supermercato.

(Più tardi...)

Kate   Ecco la spesa! Ho comprato molto: prosciutto, formaggio, pane e burro, e – francobolli per l'Inghilterra.

Tom   Niente birre? niente vino? niente per me? Uffa!

Let's speak Italian

🔊 CD2, tr 1

Over to you! If you have the recording, use it to check your answers. Always answer out loud. Start with a ten-point warm-up. Say in Italian:

1 Now we must go.
2 I would like to do the shopping.
3 Are the shops open?
4 I am sorry, but it is too expensive.
5 Is there a bus for the centre?
6 We have eaten at Mario's.
7 Can we buy wine in the supermarket?
8 It costs €37.
9 We have been here from three to half past four.
10 Damn, the bottle is broken!

Answer in Italian using **No**. Speak about yourself.

11 Ha bisogno di un Bancomat?
12 Ha visto il calcio in televisione?
13 Ha comprato tutto in farmacia?

Answer in Italian using the words in brackets.

14 Cosa ha comprato? (niente)
15 Quando va al calcio? (oggi, alle due)
16 Fino a che ora è aperto? (fino alle nove)
17 Chi ha mangiato troppo? (noi)
18 Dove ha visto la valigia? (un negozio)
19 Ha comprato qui i francobolli? (no, alla posta)
20 Che tempo fa oggi? (brutto, freddo)

Answers

1 Adesso dobbiamo andare.
2 Vorrei fare spese.
3 Sono aperti i negozi?
4 Mi dispiace, ma è troppo caro.
5 C'è un autobus per il centro?
6 Abbiamo mangiato da Mario.
7 Possiamo comprare vino nel supermercato?
8 Costa trentasette euro.
9 Siamo stati qui dalle tre alle quattro e mezza.
10 Uffa! La bottiglia è rotta!
11 No, non ho bisogno di un Bancomat.
12 No, non ho visto il calcio in televisione.
13 No, non ho comprato tutto in farmacia.
14 Non ho comprato niente.
15 Vado oggi, alle due.
16 È aperto fino alle nove.
17 Noi abbiamo mangiato troppo.
18 Ho visto la valigia in un negozio.
19 No, ho comprato i francobolli alla posta.
20 C'è brutto tempo. Fa freddo.

Let's speak more Italian

For these optional exercises add an extra 15 minutes to your daily schedule.

And remember, don't worry about getting the article or endings wrong. Near enough is good enough.

In your own words

This exercise will teach you to express yourself freely. Use only the words you have learned so far.

Tell me in your own words that...

1 you must go shopping today
2 you are aiming for the middle of the town
3 you are out of cash
4 you have to go first to a cashpoint machine ...
5 ...then you have to go to the pharmacy
6 you saw a supermarket but it was not open
7 you have to buy black shoes, size 37
8 you bought the shoes, they were a bit expensive
9 you did not buy much in the supermarket
10 you bought bread, a piece of cheese and a bottle of white wine

Answers

1 **Devo fare spese oggi.**
2 **Vado in centro.**
3 **Non ho soldi.**
4 **Prima devo passare al Bancomat...**
5 **...poi devo andare in farmacia.**
6 **Ho visto un supermercato ma non era aperto.**
7 **Devo comprare delle scarpe nere, numero trentasette.**
8 **Ho comprato le scarpe, erano un pochino care.**
9 **Non ho comprato molto al supermercato.**
10 **Ho comprato pane, un pezzo di formaggio e una bottiglia di vino bianco.**

Let's speak Italian – fast and fluently

🔊 CD2, tr 3

Translate each section and check if it is correct, then cover up the answers and say the three or four sentences fast!

Try to say each paragraph in less than 20 seconds.

Some of the English is in 'Italian-speak' to help you.

Excuse me, are you buying a television?
Is it expensive, the blue television?
No, not too much, in England it costs the same.

Scusi, compra una televisione?
È cara la televisione blu?
No, non troppo, in Inghilterra costa lo stesso.

We would like to buy a suitcase.
We have a suitcase but it (feminine) is too small.
I've seen a red suitcase but it is too expensive.

Vorremmo comprare una valigia.
Abbiamo una valigia, ma è troppo piccola.
Ho visto una valigia rossa, ma è troppo cara.

The weather was bad in April.
I was in Venice. I ate in the town centre.
The restaurant was very expensive – 300 euros.
The waiter wasn't handsome but he was nice.

C'era brutto tempo in aprile.
Ero a Venezia. Ho mangiato in centro.
Il ristorante era molto caro – trecento euro.
Il cameriere non era bello ma era simpatico!

Spot the keys

🔊 CD2, tr 4

By now you can say many things in Italian. But what happens if you ask a question and don't understand the answer – hitting you at the speed of a machine gun? The smart way is not to panic, but to listen only for the words you know. Any familiar words that you pick up will provide you with **Key words** – clues to what the other person is saying.

If you have the recording, listen to the dialogue. If you don't – read on.

You　　　 **Scusi, dov'è la posta per favore?**

An Italian　*È moltofacile,* **prima sempre diritto,** *finoalprossimoincrocio,* **dove c'è** *quel* **grande magazzino bianco. Poi a sinistra** *c'èunasiloeuna* **tintoria** *eppropriovicinoalla banca* **c'è la posta!**

Can you find your way with the key words? I think you'll get there!

Test your progress

Translate the following sentences in writing. Then check the answers and be amazed by your progress.

1 First, I would like to go to the cashpoint machine.
2 In this shop the shoes cost too much.
3 Did you see my husband in the pharmacy?
4 We were here until a quarter past ten.
5 We saw the tennis in England, on (in) television.
6 I am sorry, we do not have the same in red in size 44.
7 This shop is not cheap.
8 Who repaired my telephone? You?
9 Here is the department store. But it is not open.
10 Today we did not buy too much, only bread and half a kilo of butter.
11 I ate everything – eggs, apples, potatoes and a piece of cheese.
12 We must do the shopping. Is this the centre?
13 Yesterday I was in the office until nine o'clock.
14 The English newspapers cost a lot in Italy.
15 Is there a bus? No? It does not matter.
16 He was a very nice sales assistant.
17 What is this? Something for us?
18 Did she buy the bag near here (here near) or at the UPIM?
19 Everything was very expensive. Therefore I did not buy anything.
20 We need three kilos I believe.

Remember to fill in the **Progress chart**. You are now halfway home!

Week 4

Day-by-day guide

Study 35 minutes a day but if you are keen try 40 or even 45.

Day one

- Read **Let's go and eat**.
- Listen to/Read **Andiamo a mangiare**.
- Read the **New words**. Learn the easy ones.

Day two

- Repeat the dialogue. Learn the harder **New words**.
- Cut out the **Flash words** to help you.

Day three

- Learn all the **New words** until you know them well.
- Read and learn the **Good news grammar**.

Day four

- Cut out and learn the **Flash sentences**.
- Listen to/Read **Learn by heart**.

Day five

- Read **Say it simply**.
- Listen to/Read **Let's speak Italian**.

Day six

- Listen to/Read **Spot the keys**.
- Listen to/Read **Let's speak more Italian** (optional).
- Listen to/Read **Let's speak Italian – fast and fluently** (optional).
- Translate **Test your progress**.

Day seven

Are you keeping your scores above 60%? If so, have a well-earned day off.

Let's go and eat

Tom and Kate off to dinner with an important client. Will Kate be able to handle the infamous Edith?

No more 'Italian-speak'. As you'll have realized by now not everything can be translated word for word from one language to the other. If you simply exchange the words people may understand you and might even be amused, but saying things the Italian way will sound much better and will impress the locals.

Kate Tom, someone has telephoned. He did not say why. Signor Verdi from Milan. Here is the number.

Tom Ah yes, Bruno Verdi, a good client. His firm is in Milan. I know him well, he is very nice. I have an appointment with him on Thursday. It is an important matter.

Tom *(Telephones...)* Hello! Good morning Mr Verdi. I am Tom Walker... Yes, thank you... yes, sure, it is possible... of course... next week, very interesting... no, we have time. Wonderful! No, only two days... ah yes... when? Tonight, at eight... upstairs, by the exit... in front of the door... All right! In that case, until tonight, thank you very much, goodbye.

Kate What are we doing tonight?

Tom We are going to eat with Mr Verdi. In the centre, behind the church. He says that it is a new and very good restaurant. Mr Verdi is in Florence for three days with Edith and Peter Palmer from our company.

Kate I know Edith Palmer. She is boring and believes she knows everything. She has a terrible dog. Well... I believe I am sick. A bad cold and pains. I need a doctor.

Tom No, please. One cannot do that. Mr Verdi is very important.

(At the restaurant, Luigi, the head waiter, explains the menu.)

Luigi The fish is not on the menu and for dessert today there is tiramisu or some ice cream.

Bruno Mrs Walker, can I help you? Perhaps some pasta and afterwards meat?

Kate A steak with salad please.

Edith A steak, Kate? It is too much red meat!

Bruno And you, Mr Walker, what are you having? And what would you like to drink?

Andiamo a mangiare

🔊 CD2, tr 5

Tom and Kate are off to dinner with an important client. Will Kate be able to handle the infamous Edith?

Kate   Tom, ha telefonato qualcuno. Non ha detto perché. Il Signor Verdi di Milano. Ecco il numero.

Tom   Ah sì, Bruno Verdi, un buon cliente. La sua ditta è a Milano. Lo conosco bene, è molto simpatico. Ho un appuntamento con lui giovedì. È una cosa importante.

Tom   (Telefona...) Pronto! Buongiorno Signor Verdi. Sono Tom Walker... Sì, grazie... sì, certo, è possibile... naturalmente... la settimana prossima, molto interessante... no, abbiamo tempo. Benissimo!... No, solo due giorni... ah sì... quando? Stasera, alle otto... su, all'uscita... davanti alla porta... Va bene! Dunque, a stasera, grazie mille, arrivederci.

Kate   Cosa facciamo stasera?

Tom   Andiamo a mangiare con il Signor Verdi. In centro, dietro alla chiesa. Dice che è un ristorante nuovo e molto buono. Il Signor Verdi è a Firenze per tre giorni con Edith e Peter Palmer della nostra ditta.

Kate   Conosco Edith Palmer. È noiosa e crede di sapere tutto. Ha un cane terribile. Beh... Credo di essere malata. Un brutto raffreddore e dolori. Ho bisogno del medico...

Tom   No, per favore! Non si può fare! Il Signor Verdi è molto importante.

(Al ristorante, Luigi, il cameriere, spiega il menù.)

Luigi   Il pesce non è sul menù e come dessert oggi c'è il tiramisù o del gelato.

Bruno   Signora Walker, posso aiutarla? Forse della pasta e dopo carne?

Kate   Una bistecca con insalata per favore.

Edith   Una bistecca, Kate? È troppa carne rossa!

Bruno   E Lei, Signor Walker, cosa prende? E cosa desidera bere?

Tom   A veal cutlet 'alla Milanese' with chips and vegetables, and a beer, please.

Edith   There is a lot of oil in the vegetables, Tom.

Bruno   And you, Mrs Palmer?

Edith   I take some chicken and a glass of water, please.

(Later...)

Bruno   Are we having fruit, or perhaps better – the tiramisu? No? Nothing? Have we finished? A coffee for someone? Nobody? Good, the bill, please.

Edith   Mr Verdi, please help me! How does one say 'doggy bag' in Italian? I would like a little meat for my dog.

Kate   But Edith, the dog is in England!

Tom Una cotoletta alla milanese con patatine e verdura, e una birra, per favore.

Edith C'è molto olio nella verdura, Tom.

Bruno E Lei, Signora Palmer?

Edith Prendo del pollo e un bicchiere d'acqua, per favore.

(Più tardi...)

Bruno Prendiamo della frutta, o forse meglio – il tiramisù? No? Niente? Abbiamo finito? Un caffè per qualcuno? Nessuno? Bene, il conto, per favore!

Edith Signor Verdi, mi aiuti per favore! Come si dice in italiano 'doggy bag'? Vorrei un po' di carne per il mio cane.

Kate Ma Edith, il cane è in Inghilterra!

New words

🔊 CD2, tr 6

qualcuno someone
ha detto he/she/it has said, you said
perché why, because
signor Mr, gentleman
il cliente the client
il suo, la sua his/her *(agrees with noun)*
conosco I know
bene well, *also: good!*
appuntamento appointment
con lui *with him*
giovedì Thursday
una cosa a matter, a thing
importante important
pronto! ready *(and what you say when you answer the phone)*
grazie, grazie mille thank you, many (a thousand) thanks
certo sure, certain
possible possible
naturalmente of course
la settimana prossima next week
interessante interesting
benissimo very good, excellent
su *up, upstairs, also on*
uscita exit
davanti a in front of, before
porta door
stasera tonight
facciamo we do, make
dietro a behind
chiesa church
dice he/she/it says, you say

che that
il ristorante the restaurant
nostro/a our
crede he/she/it believes, you believe
sapere to know
il cane the dog
terribile terrible
malato/a sick, ill
un raffreddore a cold
dolori pains
medico doctor
non si può fare one can't do that, that's not on
il pesce the fish
il menu the menu
come like, as
gelato ice cream
posso I can
aiutare to help
la carne the meat
bistecca steak
insalata salad
prende you take, he/she/it takes
desidera you would like, he/she/it would like
cotoletta alla Milanese veal cutlet 'alla milanese'
le patatine the chips
verdura vegetables
olio oil
prendo I take
pollo chicken
il bicchiere the glass

acqua water
frutta fruit
meglio better
finito finished

nessuno nobody
mi aiuti, per favore help me, please
come si dice in italiano? how
    do you say … in Italian?

> **TOTAL NEW WORDS: 67**
> **…only 94 words to go!**

Last easy extras
I giorni della settimana (*the days of the week*)

lunedì	*Monday*	**venerdì**	*Friday*
martedì	*Tuesday*	**sabato**	*Saturday*
mercoledì	*Wednesday*	**domenica**	*Sunday*
giovedì	*Thursday*		

Good news grammar

🔊 CD2, tr 7

1 The past: team players and rebels

Remember **comprare**, **mangiare** and **riparare**? They all end in **-are**.

Let's call them team players, because when you use them in the past, to say that you *did* or *have done something*, they all end in **-ato**: **ho comprato/mangiato/riparato**.

Here are three more team players:

lavorare	→	**lavorato**
aiutare	→	**aiutato**
telefonare	→	**telefonato**

Then there are a couple of players from a neighbouring team. They end in **-ere** and finish up with **-uto** in the past.

conoscere	*(to know)*	→	**conosciuto** *(known)*
credere	*(to believe)*	→	**creduto** *(believed)*

Finally the rebels: relax, there are only five.

dire	*(to say)*	→	**detto** *(said)*
prendere	*(to take)*	→	**preso** *(taken)*
fare	*(to do)*	→	**fatto** *(done)*
vedere	*(to see)*	→	**visto** *(seen)*
scrivere	*(to write)*	→	**scritto** *(written)*

Spend ten minutes practising these past forms. It's quite simple once you use them.

> **Chi lo ha detto?** *(Who has said it?)*
> **Cosa abbiamo preso?** *(What have we taken?)*
> **Cosa ha fatto?** *(What has he/she done?)*
> **Ha visto Luigi?** *(Did you/he/she see Luigi?)*
> **Ho scritto a Maria.** *(I have written to Maria.)*

Remember, if you ever 'lose' a verb or verb form, you'll find it in the verb summary, in Week 6.

2 'It' and 'them'

Imagine you are talking about things – *wine*, *the company*, *holidays* or *seats on the plane*. Now imagine you are referring to these things. You would say *it* or *them*.

In Italian *it* is **lo** or **la**, and *them* is **li** or **le**, depending on whether the things you are referring to are masculine or feminine, or one thing or more.

Compro *vino.*	***Lo* compro.**	*I buy it.*
Compra *la ditta.*	***La* compra.**	*You/he/she/buys it.*
Ha *le vacanze* **in aprile.**	***Le* ha in aprile.**	*He has them in April.*
Abbiamo *posti.*	***Li* abbiamo.**	*We have them.*

Did you notice that *it* or *them* always goes in front of the verb?

   It *I buy.* ***It*** *you buy.* ***Them*** *we have.*

3 Last quick verb box – *dovere:* 'must, have to'

Three minutes should do it, now you know the pattern.

> **devo – deve – dobbiamo – devono**

Learn by heart

🔊 CD2, tr 8

Here is a short piece about someone who is rather fed up. Put yourself in his shoes. Learn it and act it out in under 50 seconds.

Non mi piace...

A   **Conosce il Signor Martini?**
    Ha telefonato ieri. Devo andare a mangiare con lui.

B   **Perché?**

A   **È un buon cliente della ditta.**
    Però non è simpatico – mangia e beve troppo.

B   **E quando?**

A   **Stasera! C'è il calcio in televisione.**
    Vorrei dire che sono malato... ma non posso...
    Sempre la ditta...!

B   **Ah... mi dispiace!**

Say it simply

When people want to speak Italian but don't dare, it's usually because they are trying to translate what they want to say from English into Italian. But because they don't know some of the words, they give up!

With **Traveller's Italian** you work around the words you don't know by using the words you do know! And believe me, around 400 words are enough to say anything!

It may not always be very elegant, but who cares? The important thing is you're speaking, communicating!

Here are three examples, showing you how to say things in a simple way. The English words which are not part of the *'fast-track'* vocabulary have been highlighted.

1 You need to **change your flight** to London from Tuesday to Friday.

This is what you could say – simply:

Non possiamo andare martedì, vorremmo andare venerdì.
We cannot go Tuesday, we would like to go Friday.

or:

Martedì non va bene per noi. Venerdì è meglio.
Tuesday is not good for us. Friday is better.

2 You want to get your **purse** from the coach, which the driver has locked.

Say it simply:

Mi dispiace. I miei soldi sono sull'autobus.
I am sorry. My money is in the bus.

or:

Ho bisogno di qualcosa importante. Mi dispiace molto, ma tutto è sull'autobus. *I need something important. I am very sorry but everything is in the bus.*

3 This time your friend has **just broken** the **heel** of her only pair of shoes. You have to catch a train and need some help now.

This is what you could say:

Scusi, la scarpa è rotta, e abbiamo poco tempo. C'è un negozio qui dove riparano le scarpe al momento?
Excuse me, the shoe is broken and we have little time. Is there a shop here where they repair the shoes at the moment?

Let's speak Italian

x

🔊 CD2, tr 9

Here are eight sentences to say in Italian, and then on to greater things!

1 I am sorry, I do not have time.
2 Are we going with him?
3 I would like a salad.
4 We have been here yesterday.
5 Excuse me, what did you say?
6 I did not take this.
7 When did you work in Italy?
8 We did not do anything.

Now pretend you are in Italy with English friends who do not speak Italian. They will want you to ask people things and will want you to do it for them in Italian. They will say: *Please ask him...* Start with **Scusi...**

9 ...if he has seen Mr Rossi.
10 ...where he bought the stamps.
11 ...if he has an appointment now.
12 ...where the restaurant is.

Now your friends will ask you to tell someone things. They use some words which you don't know, so you have to work round it by using the once you do. Your friends will say: *Please tell her that...* Start your sentence with **Mi dispiace, ma...**

13 ...her pasta is cold.
14 ...we are not having wine, only water.
15 ...she is a vegetarian.
16 ...he does not have his number.

While shopping you are offered various items. You take them all, *saying Yes, I take it* or *Yes, I take them*.

17 ...e la frutta?
18 ...e i gelati?
19 ...e le birre?
20 ...e il vino?

Answers

1 Mi dispiace, non ho tempo.
2 Andiamo con lui?
3 Vorrei un'insalata.
4 Siamo stati (*or* state) qui ieri.
5 Scusi, cosa ha detto?
6 Non ho preso questo.
7 Quando ha lavorato in Italia?
8 Non abbiamo fatto niente.
9 Scusi, ha visto il Signor Rossi?
10 Scusi, dove ha comprato i francobolli?
11 Scusi, ha un appuntamento adesso?
12 Scusi, dov'è il ristorante?
13 Mi dispiace, ma la sua pasta è fredda.
14 Mi dispiace, ma non abbiamo vino, solo acqua.
15 Mi dispiace, ma non mangia carne.
16 Mi dispiace, ma non ha il suo numero.
17 Sì, la prendo.
18 Sì, li prendo.
19 Sì, le prendo.
20 Sì, lo prendo.

Let's speak more Italian

🔊 CD2, tr 10

In your own words

This exercise will teach you to express yourself freely. Use only the words you have learned so far. Where possible speak for yourself and a friend.

Tell me in your own words that...

1 somebody telephoned – it was Mr Verdi
2 you have an appointment with him next week
3 he works for a firm in Milan
4 he is a good client
5 you (plural) are going to eat in a new restaurant
6 you've got a bad cold – you need a doctor
7 you haven't got time to go to the doctor
8 you can go to the chemist
9 you'd like a steak with potatoes and salad
10 you went home at half past eleven

Answers

1 **Ha telefonato qualcuno – era il Signor Verdi.**
2 **Ho un appuntamento con lui la settimana prossima.**
3 **Lavora per una ditta a Milano.**
4 **È un buon cliente.**
5 **Andiamo a mangiare in un ristorante nuovo.**
6 **Ho un brutto raffreddore – ho bisogno del medico.**
7 **Non abbiamo tempo di andare dal medico.**
8 **Possiamo andare in farmacia.**
9 **Vorrei una bistecca con patate e insalata.**
10 **Siamo andati a casa alle undici e mezza.**

Let's speak Italian – fast and fluently

◀) CD2, tr 11

Translate each section and check if it is correct, then cover up the answers and say the three or four sentences fast!

Try to say each section in less than 20 seconds.

Do you know Bruno Verdi? He phoned yesterday.
Why? He said it was important.
The appointment in Florence was on Wednesday.

Conosce Bruno Verdi? Ha telefonato ieri.
Perché? Ha detto che era importante.
L'appuntamento a Firenze era mercoledì.

Bruno is in Florence for three days.
There is a very good restaurant behind the church.
Bruno says it's expensive.

Bruno è a Firenze per tre giorni.
C'è un ristorante molto buono dietro alla chiesa.
Bruno dice che è caro.

Unfortunately, I can't go to the restaurant.
My dog is ill. He has eaten too much meat.
Oh, I am very sorry. How do you say in Italian: 'Poor little thing?'
(poveretto)

Purtroppo, non posso andare al ristorante.
Il mio cane è malato. Ha mangiato troppa carne.
Oh, mi dispiace. Come si dice in italiano 'Poor little thing'?
'Poveretto.'

Spot the keys

🔊 CD2, tr 12

You practised listening for key words when you asked the way to the post office in Week 3. Now you are in a department store. You have asked the sales assistant if the black shoes you liked are also available in size 44 (Italian).

She said **no** then **un momento, per favore** and disappeared. When she came back this is what she said:

Ho appena guardato in magazzino se ne rimaneva **una nella sua taglia, ma c'è solo in verde. Ma questo** *modello è tagliato piuttosto* **grande,** *quindi* **credo che la taglia quarantadue** *possa* **andare bene per Lei.**

It appears that size 44 was only available in green but she felt that size 42 might be big enough.

Test your progress

1 Did you say that somebody has telephoned? Signor Gucci?
2 I would like to know where the restaurants are.
3 It is late and he is not there. What are we doing tonight?
4 Here is the menu! Do you know the wines of (the) Tuscany?
5 The cash dispenser is upstairs, behind the exit, near the door.
6 Wednesday we must go to the doctor. It is an important appointment.
7 Why do you say she is boring? Because I know her well.
8 Have you seen him? I must go to Pisa with him.
9 (The) Signor Rossini is my client. He has bought everything.
10 I would like to buy this thing. How does one say in Italian…?
11 Next week? I am sorry. It is not possible.
12 There is too much. Please help me. Many thanks!
13 Eighty euros for two days? Very interesting. Yes, of course we take it.
14 I must buy three things for my friends.
15 He says that he has a (the) cold and that he has not finished his work.
16 Can they eat only the minestrone?
17 Please help me. There is a terrible dog.
18 Nobody has seen who has eaten the steak.
19 Can I say something: the chicken is not bad, but the fish is better.
20 What do you take? The fruit? Yes, sure, it is from (the) Tuscany.

If you are happy with your result take it straight to the **Progress chart**.

Week 5

Day-by-day guide

How about 15 minutes on the train, tube or bus, 10 minutes on the way home and 20 minutes before switching on the television...?

Day one

- Read **On the move**.
- Listen to/Read **In viaggio**.
- Read the **New words**. Learn 15 or more.

Day two

- Repeat **In viaggio** and the **New words**.
- Cut out the **Flash words** and get stuck in.

Day three

- Test yourself to perfection on all the **New words**.
- Listen to/Read **Learn by heart**.

Day four

- Read and learn the **Good news grammar**.
- Cut out and learn the **Flash sentences**.

Day five

- Listen to/Read **Let's speak Italian**.
- Listen to/Read **Spot the keys**.

Day six

- Listen to/Read **Let's speak more Italian** (optional).
- Listen to/Read **Let's speak Italian – fast and fluently** (optional).
- Translate **Test your progress**.

Day seven

How is the Progress chart looking? Great?... Great! I bet you don't want a day off... but I insist!

On the move

Tom and Kate travel through the lakes of Northern Italy by train, bus and hire car.

(At the station...)

Tom   Two tickets for Como, please.

Clerk   Thereandback?

Tom   There and what? Can you speak more slowly please?

Clerk   There – and – back?

Tom   No, one way only. At what time is there a train and from which platform?

Clerk   At 9.56. Platform eight.

Kate   Quickly Tom, here are two seats, non-smoking*. Oh, but someone is smoking. Excuse me, you (one) cannot smoke, because it is non-smoking here. It is forbidden to smoke.

Man   I am sorry. I don't understand. I speak only English.

(At the bus stop...)

Kate   There is no bus. We have to wait 20 minutes. Tom, here are my postcards. Over there is a letterbox. I would like to take some photos. The lake is beautiful with the sun.

Tom   Kate, quickly! There are a lot of people. Here are two buses! Both are blue. This one is full. Let's take the other one. *(On the bus...)* Two for Milan, please.

Driver   This bus goes only to Como.

Tom   But we are in Como!

Driver   Yes, yes, but this is the bus for the hospital of Como.

(In the car...)

Tom   Here is our car. Only €40 for three days. I am very pleased.

Kate   I do not like the car. It costs so little because it is very old. Let's hope that we don't have problems.

*Please note that smoking is no longer permitted in any compartment on Italian

trains.

In viaggio

🔊 CD2, tr 15

Tom and Kate travel through the lakes of Northern Italy by train, bus and hire car.

(Alla stazione...)

Tom   Due biglietti per Como, per favore.

Clerk   Andataeritorno?

Tom   Andata e cosa? Può parlare più lentamente per favore.

Clerk   Andata – e – ritorno?

Tom   No, solo andata. A che ora c'è un treno e da che binario?

Clerk   Alle nove e cinquantasei. Binario otto.

Kate   Presto Tom, qui ci sono due posti 'non fumatori'*. Oh, ma qualcuno fuma. Scusi, non si può fumare, perché qui è'non fumatori'. È proibito fumare.

Man   I am sorry. Non capisco. Parlo only English.

(Alla fermata dell'autobus...)

Kate   Non c'è l'autobus. Dobbiamo aspettare venti minuti. Tom, ecco le mie cartoline. Là c'è una buca delle lettere. Vorrei fare delle foto. Il lago è bellissimo con il sole!

Tom   Kate, presto! C'è molta gente. Ecco due autobus! Tutti e due sono blu. Questo è pieno. Prendiamo l'altro.
(Nell' autobus...) Due per Milano per favore.

Driver   Quest'autobus va solo fino a Como.

Tom   Ma siamo a Como!

Driver   Sì, sì, ma questo è l'autobus per l'ospedale di Como.

(In auto...)

Tom   Ecco la nostra auto. Solo quaranta euro per tre giorni. Sono molto contento.

Kate   L'auto non mi piace. Costa così poco perché è molto vecchia. Speriamo di non avere problemi.

Tom   I am sorry. The first car was too expensive and the second (one) too big. This was the last one.

(Later...) Where are we? The map has disappeared! On the left there is a petrol station, and on the right there is a school. Come on, quickly!

Kate   We are coming from the underground station. The main road is at the traffic light. It's perhaps three kilometres to the motorway. *(On the motorway...)* Why does the car go so slowly? Have we enough petrol? How many litres? Do we have oil? Is the engine not too hot? They have given us a broken car. Where is the mobile phone? Where is the number of the mechanic *(garage)*? Where is my bag?

Tom   Kate, please! All this gives me a headache. And now comes also the rain! And why are the police behind us?

Tom   Mi dispiace. La prima auto era troppo cara e la seconda
            troppo grande. Questa era l'ultima.

            (Più tardi...) Dove siamo? La cartina è sparita!
            A sinistra c'è un benzinaio, e a destra c'è una scuola.
            Dai, presto!

Kate   Veniamo dalla fermata del metro. La strada principale è
            al semaforo. Sono forse tre chilometri fino all'autostrada.
            (In autostrada...) Perché l'auto va così lentamente? Abbiamo
            abbastanza benzina? Quanti litri? Abbiamo olio? Il motore
            non è troppo caldo? Ci hanno dato un'auto rotta. Dov'è il
            telefonino? Dov'è il numero del meccanico? Dov'è la mia
            borsa?

Tom   Kate, **per favore!** Tutto questo mi fa venire il mal di testa!
            E adesso viene anche la pioggia! E perché c'è la polizia dietro
            di noi?

New words

🔊 CD2, tr 14

in viaggio on the move, travelling
la stazione (railway) station
biglietto ticket
andata e ritorno return ticket ('going and returning')
parlare to speak
più more
lentamente slowly
treno train
binario track, platform
presto quick, quickly
non fumatori non-smoking
fuma he/she/it smokes, you smoke
si può/non si può one can/ one cannot
fumare to smoke
proibito forbidden
non capisco I don't understand
parlo I speak
fermata stop
aspettare to wait
cartolina postcard
buca delle lettere letterbox
la foto, le foto the photo, the photos
lago lake
bellissimo/a very beautiful
il sole the sun
la gente the people
tutti e due both ('all and two')
pieno/a full
altro/a other
l'ospedale the hospital
l'auto (la) the car

giorno, giorni day, days
contento/a pleased, happy
mi piace/non mi piace I like/I do not like
così so
vecchio/a old
speriamo we hope, let's hope
i problemi the problems
primo/a first
secondo/a second
ultimo/a last
cartina map
sparito/a disappeared
benzinaio petrol station
dai! come on!
veniamo we come, we are coming
strada principale main road
semaforo traffic light
chilometro kilometre
autostrada motorway
benzina petrol
litro, litri litre, litres
il motore the motor, engine
caldo/a hot
ci us
dare/dato give/given
meccanico mechanic (at a garage)
fa he/she/it makes, you make
venire to come
il mal di testa the headache
pioggia rain
polizia police
noi us, we

> **TOTAL NEW WORDS: 63**
> ...only 31 words to go!

Learn by heart

🔊 CD2, tr 15

Someone has crashed the car and someone else is getting suspicious. Try to say these lines fluently and like a prize-winning play!

Andiamo al tennis

A   Andiamo al tennis. Mi piacciono i due americani. Ho dei biglietti della mia ditta. Prendiamo l'autobus, o meglio, il metro. C'è anche un treno tutto il giorno.

B   L'autobus? Il metro? Un treno? Perché? Cosa c'è? Abbiamo un'auto laggiù*.

A   Beh... ieri, con la pioggia, non ho visto il semaforo. Però è poco, solo la porta, e il meccanico era molto simpatico!

*laggiù: *down there*

Good news grammar

🔊 CD2, tr 16

1 Confusing: *mi, me, Lei, gli, ci, noi, la, lo, lui, lei*

You have come across these little words in the stories and the
New words. Some appeared before the verbs: **ci hanno dato** (*they
have given us*). And some were stuck onto the end: **Posso aiutarla?**
(*Can I help you?*) or **Può farlo?** (*Can you do it?*).

Learning these words 'cold' is quite difficult, but when they come up
in the **Flash sentences** or the texts, it's not so bad. And when you
speak Italian you can muddle them up or avoid them altogether.

I have extracted six easy and useful ones. Spend five minutes learning
them and take another five minutes to remember them.

| *for me* | **per *me*** | *for him* | **per *lui*** | *for us* | **per *noi*** |
| *for you* | **per *Lei*** | *for her* | **per *lei*** | *for them* | **per *loro*** |

You use the same words with **con**, **a** and **da**:

> **con me** *with me*
> **a Lei** *to you*
>
> **da loro** *from them* or *at their house*

2 Mi piace – non mi piace

You will use this all the time. Think how often you use
I like – I don't like in English.

You can like or not like *things* or *doing things*:

> **Mi piace la sua scuola.** *I like her school.*
> **Mi piace mangiare con lui.** *I like to eat with him.*
> **Non mi piace il pesce.** *I don't like the fish.*
> **Mi piace molto.** *I like (him/her/it) a lot.*

If you like more than one thing, you say **mi piacciono**:

> **Mi piacciono i negozi.** *I like the shops.*
> **Non mi piacciono i ristoranti.** *I don't like the resaurants.*

3 A reminder: *ho bisogno*

Remember **ho bisogno** from Week 1? **Ho bisogno di molti soldi**.
It literally means *I have need of...* This is just a reminder to use it.

> **Ho bisogno di *un medico*.** *I need a doctor.*
> **Abbiamo bisogno di *un meccanico*...** *Anche noi!*
> *We need a mechanic... We, too!*

Let's speak Italian

🔊 CD2, tr 17

A ten-point warm-up: I give you an answer and you ask me a question as if you did not hear the words in CAPITAL LETTERS very well.

> *Example* **Lucia è ALLA POSTA.**
> *Ask* **Dov'è Lucia?**

1 Il telefonino è NELLA MIA BORSA.
2 Sono stato/a in ospedale IN MARZO.
3 Tom vorrebbe parlare CON MARCELLO.
4 Per Pisa, andata e ritorno costa €15.
5 Non ho visto IL SEMAFORO.
6 SÌ, sono contento della scuola.
7 NO, la cartina non mi piace.
8 Vanno in Inghilterra CON LA FERRARI.
9 La casa non mi piace PERCHÉ È MOLTO VECCHIA.
10 Le vacanze erano BELLISSIME.

Answer in Italian using *yes* or *no*. Speak about yourself.

11 Ha visto il benzinaio?
12 Prende questo treno?
13 Va adesso alla stazione?
14 Le piace il lago?
15 Può fumare qui?

Explain these words in Italian. Your answers can differ from mine.

16 an au pair
17 kennels
18 teacher
19 unemployed
20 to be broke

Answers

1 Dov'è il telefonino?
2 Quando è stato/a in ospedale?
3 Con chi vorrebbe parlare Tom?
4 Quanto costa per Pisa, andata e ritorno?
5 Cosa non ha visto?
6 È contento della scuola?
7 Le piace la cartina?
8 Come vanno in Inghilterra?
9 Perché non le piace la casa?
10 Com'erano le vacanze?
11 Sì, l'ho visto./No, non l'ho visto.
12 Sì, lo prendo. No, non lo prendo.
13 Sì, vado adesso. No, non vado adesso.
14 Sì, mi piace. No, non mi piace.
15 Sì, qui posso fumare. No, qui non posso fumare.
16 Una signora che aiuta in casa con tutto il lavoro.
17 Una casa per il cane quando siamo in vacanza.
18 Qualcuno che lavora nella scuola con i bambini.
19 Qualcuno che non ha lavoro.
20 Non abbiamo più soldi. Sono finiti.

Let's speak more Italian

CD2, tr 18

In your own words

This exercise will teach you to express yourself freely. Use only the words you have learned so far.

Tell me in your own words that ...

1 you bought a return ticket to Como
2 there is a train at 10.15 from platform eight
3 it is forbidden, but somebody is smoking in a non-smoking seat
4 on Monday you would like to go to Milan by bus
5 you must take some photos for your mother
6 this bus is packed; you *(pl.)* are going to take the other one
7 the car is cheap because it is very old
8 your wife says: 'They have given us a broken car'
9 the car goes so slowly and the engine overheats
10 hopefully you won't have problems

Answers

1 Ho comprato un biglietto di andata e ritorno per Como.
2 C'è un treno alle dieci e un quarto dal binario otto.
3 È proibito, ma qualcuno fuma in un posto 'non fumatori'.
4 Lunedì vorrei andare a Milano in autobus.
5 Devo fare delle foto per mia madre.
6 Questo autobus è pieno. Prendiamo l'altro.
7 L'auto costa poco perché è molto vecchia.
8 Mia moglie dice: 'Ci hanno dato un'auto rotta.'
9 L'auto va così lentamente e il motore è troppo caldo.
10 Speriamo di non avere problemi.

Let's speak Italian – fast and fluently

◀) CD2, tr 19

Translate each section and check if it is correct, then cover up the answers and say the three or four sentences fast. Try to beat 20 seconds.

A ticket to Milan, please, only one way.
How much? €21? Can you speak more slowly, please?
Thank you. When does the train leave?

Un biglietto per Milano, per favore, solo andata.
Quanto? Ventun euro? Può parlare più lentamente, per favore?
Grazie. A che ora parte il treno?

We would like to take the bus.
We have to wait twenty minutes.
We can take a photo of the lake.

Vorremmo prendere l'autobus.
Dobbiamo aspettare venti minuti.
Possiamo fare una foto del lago.

We don't have a map of Italy.
It's ten kilometres to the motorway.
The traffic light is red.
We have a problem. Perhaps our car is broken.
My wife has a headache.

Non abbiamo una cartina dell'Italia.
Sono dieci chilometri fino all'autostrada.
Il semaforo è rosso.
Abbiamo un problema. Forse la nostra auto è rotta.
Mia moglie ha mal di testa.

Spot the keys

🔊 CD2, tr 20

This time you plan a trip in the country and wonder about the weather.

You   **Scusi, vorrei sapere che tempo fa.**

Answer   **Non so cosa** *dicano le previsioni* **in televisione** *ma mi sembra di avere capito che c'è una perturbazione che arriva. Farà ancora piuttosto* **caldo, più o meno venticinque** *gradi, ma prima di* **stasera** *avremo sicuramente della* **pioggia.**

He doesn't know something on television (?) but you heard the word *hot* and then *more* or *less 25* (degrees centigrade). You also understood *this evening* and *rain*. Perhaps you'd better take an umbrella!

Test your progress

1 It is forbidden to go to the restaurant without shoes.
2 I like your Lamborghini. Was it very cheap?
3 When I am travelling (on the move) I always speak a lot of Italian.
4 I need six tickets. Are there non-smoking seats?
5 Let's hope we don't have (not to have) problems with the engine.
6 I do not like the Internet. It is difficult. I believe I am (to be) too old.
7 I do not understand. Can you speak more slowly, please?
8 It is hot and there are a lot of people here. Let's go to the lake.
9 One hour with her gives me (me makes come) a (the) headache.
10 There is a bus at the traffic lights. Where is it going?
11 The credit card has (is) disappeared. We have to telephone the police.
12 Let's do it like this: first we buy the Ferrari for me and afterwards a T-shirt for you.
13 I like this car, but the other (one) was better.
14 We have only a litre of petrol and there is not a petrol station until Naples.
15 I like the sun and I like the rain. I like both.
16 *(On the phone)* Hello, we are 20 km from Pisa. Is there a mechanic?
17 Excuse me, can you help me, please? I do not know Rome. Where is the station?
18 The main street? It is not difficult if you take the metro.
19 Where are they? What have they done? I do not like to wait.
20 We are coming from (the) platform 17. Where is Mario?

If you know all the words, you should score over 90%.

Week 6

Day-by-day guide

This is your last week! Need I say more?

Day one

- Read **In the airport**.
- Listen to/Read **In aeroporto**.
- Read the **New words**. There are only 31!

Day two

- Repeat **In aeroporto** and learn all the **New words**.
- Work with the **Flash words** and **Flash sentences**.

Day three

- Test yourself on the **Flash sentences**.
- No more **Good news grammar**! Have a look at the summary.

Day four

- Listen to/Read and learn **Arrivederci**!
- Read **Say it simply**.

Day five

- Listen to/Read **Spot the keys**.
- Listen to/Read **Let's speak Italian**.

Day six

- Listen to/Read **Let's speak more Italian** (optional).
- Listen to/Read **Let's speak Italian – fast and fluently** (optional).
- Your last **Test your progress**! Go for it!

Day seven

> **Congratulations!**
> **You have successfully completed the course and**
> **can now speak**
> ***Traveller's Italian***

In the airport

It's the end of the trip and time to go home. There's one more surprise for Tome and Kate when they bump into an old friend in the departure lounge.

Tom On Monday we must work. Terrible. I would rather go to Miami or Honolulu. Nobody knows where I am and the office can wait.

Kate And *my* company? What do they do? They speak with my mother. She has the number of my mobile. And then?

Tom Yes, yes, I know (it). Well, perhaps at Christmas we'll go for a week in the snow or to Madeira on a ship... There is a kiosk down there. I'll go and buy a newspaper... Kate, there is Gino Pavarotti!

Gino Hello! How are you? What are you doing here? This is my wife, Nancy. Are the holidays over? How were they?

Kate Italy is wonderful. We have seen a lot and eaten too much. Now we know Tuscany and the lakes very well.

Gino Next year Venice! What a fantastic city!... Mrs Walker, my wife would like to buy a book about computers. Can you go with her and help her, please? Mr Walker, you have the newspaper. Are there any photos of the football? And then are we going to drink something?

(At the kiosk...)

Kate There is nothing here. I do not see anything of interest. Are you also going to England?

Nancy No, we are going to Pisa to Gino's mother. Our children are often with her during the holidays. Tomorrow we'll take the train. It costs less.

Kate Your husband works at the Bank of Italy?

In aeroporto

🔊 CD2, tr 21

It's the end of the trip and time to go home. There's one more surprise for Tome and Kate when they bump into an old friend in the departure lounge.

Tom   Lunedì dobbiamo lavorare. Terribile. Vorrei invece andare a Miami o a Honolulu. Nessuno sa dove sono e la ditta può aspettare.

Kate   E la *mia* ditta? Cosa fanno? Parlano con mia madre. Lei ha il numero del mio telefonino. E poi…?

Tom   Sì, sì, lo so. Allora, forse a Natale andiamo una settimana sulla neve o a Madeira in nave… C'è un chiosco laggiù. Vado a comprare un giornale… Kate, c'è Gino Pavarotti!

Gino   Salve! Come va? Cosa fa qui? Questa è mia moglie, Nancy. Sono finite le vacanze? Come sono state?

Kate   L'Italia è meravigliosa. Abbiamo visto molto e mangiato troppo. Adesso conosciamo la Toscana e i laghi molto bene.

Gino   Il prossimo anno Venezia! Che città fantastica!… Signora Walker, mia moglie vorrebbe comprare un libro di computer. Per favore, può andare con lei e aiutarla? Signor Walker, Lei ha il giornale. Ci sono delle foto del calcio? E poi andiamo a bere qualcosa?

(Al chiosco…)

Kate   Qui non c'è niente. Non vedo niente di interessante. Va anche Lei in Inghilterra?

Nancy   No, andiamo a Pisa dalla madre di Gino. I nostri bambini sono spesso da lei durante le vacanze. Domani prendiamo il treno. Costa meno.

Kate   Suo marito lavora alla Banca d'Italia?

Nancy Yes. The work is interesting, but the money is little. We have an apartment (which is) too small for us and an old car. It always needs a lot of repairs. My family lives in California and my girlfriend is in Florida and we write a lot of e-mails. I would like to go to America but it is too expensive.

Kate But you have a beautiful house in Portofino.

Nancy A house in Portofino? I have never been to Portofino. When we have holidays we go to a friend in Genoa.

Tom Kate, come on, quickly. We must go. Goodbye. What is the matter, Kate? What did Mrs Pavarotti say?

Kate Wait, Tom, wait...

Nancy Sì. Il lavoro è interessante, ma i soldi sono pochi. Abbiamo un appartamento troppo piccolo per noi e una vecchia auto. Ha bisogno sempre di molte riparazioni. La mia famiglia vive in California e la mia amica è in Florida e ci scriviamo molte e-mail. Vorrei andare in America ma costa troppo.

Kate Ma Lei ha una bella casa a Portofino.

Nancy Una casa a Portofino? Non sono mai stata a Portofino. Quando abbiamo le vacanze andiamo a Genova da un amico.

Tom Kate, dai, presto. Dobbiamo andare. Arrivederci. Che cosa c'è, Kate? Cosa ha detto la Signora Pavarotti?

Kate Aspetta,Tom, aspetta...

New words

🔊 CD2, tr 22

aeroporto airport

invece (di) instead (of), on the other hand

la madre the mother

sa he/she/it knows, you know

fanno they do, make

parlano they speak

lo so I know it

Natale Christmas

la neve the snow

la nave the ship

chiosco kiosk

laggiù down there

salve hello *(not quite as familiar as ciao)*

come va? how are you?

meraviglioso/a wonderful

conosciamo we know

città town, city

fantastico/a fantastic

vorrebbe he/she/it/you would like

libro book

vedo I see

durante during

spesso often

appartamento apartment, flat

le riparazioni the repairs

famiglia family

vive he/she/it lives, you live

scriviamo we write

mai never, ever

che cosa c'è? what's the matter?

aspetta! wait!

TOTAL NEW WORDS: 31
Total ITALIAN words learned: 379
Extra words: 79
GRAND TOTAL: 458

Learn by heart

🔊 CD2, tr 23

This is your last dialogue to learn by heart. Give it your best! You now have a large store of everyday sayings which will be very useful.

Arrivederci…!

Kate Pronto. Buongiorno Signor Verdi. Sono Kate Walker.
Siamo all'aeroporto. Sì, le vacanze sono finite.
Che bella, l'Italia!
Tom vorrebbe parlare con Lei. Un momento per favore
e… arrivederci!

Tom Ciao, Bruno! Cosa? Ha comprato tutti e due?
C'è un'e-mail della ditta?
Benissimo! Mille grazie!
L'anno prossimo? Kate vorrebbe andare a Capri,
ma io vorrei vedere* Venezia.
Con Edith Palmer? *Per favore!*
Dobbiamo andare. Dunque… a presto! Ciao! Arrivederci!

*vedere: *(to)* see*

Good news grammar

As promised, there is no new grammar in this lesson, just a summary of all the verbs which appear in the six weeks. The 31 verbs are not for learning, just for a quick check. You know and have used most of them!

Basic form	I	you, he, she, it	we	they	Past
avere	ho	ha	abbiamo	hanno	avuto
aiutare	aiuto	aiuta	aiutiamo	aiutano	aiutato
andare	vado	va	andiamo	vanno	(sono) andato
aspettare	aspetto	aspetta	aspettiamo	aspettano	aspettato
bere	bevo	beve	beviamo	bevono	bevuto
capire	capisco	capisce	capiamo	capiscono	capito
comprare	compro	compra	compriamo	comprano	comprato
conoscere	conosco	conosce	conosciamo	conoscono	conosciuto
costare		costa		costano	
credere	credo	crede	crediamo	credono	creduto
dare	do	dà	diamo	danno	dato
desiderare	desidero	desidera	desideriamo	desiderano	desiderato
dire	dico	dice	diciamo	dicono	detto
dovere	devo	deve	dobbiamo	devono	dovuto
essere	sono	è	siamo	sono	(sono) stato
(imperf.)	ero	era	eravamo	erano	
fare	faccio	fa	facciamo	fanno	fatto
fumare	fumo	fuma	fumiamo	fumano	fumato
lavorare	lavoro	lavora	lavoriamo	lavorano	lavorato
mangiare	mangio	mangia	mangiamo	mangiano	mangiato
parlare	parlo	parla	parliamo	parlano	parlato
passare	passo	passa	passiamo	passano	passato
potere	posso	può	possiamo	possono	potuto
prendere	prendo	prende	prendiamo	prendono	preso
riparare	riparo	ripara	ripariamo	riparano	riparato
sapere	so	sa	sappiamo	sanno	saputo
scrivere	scrivo	scrive	scriviamo	scrivono	scritto
sperare	spero	spera	speriamo	sperano	sperato
telefonare	telefono	telefona	telefoniamo	telefonano	telefonato
vedere	vedo	vede	vediamo	vedono	visto
venire	vengo	viene	veniamo	vengono	sono venuto
(volere)	vorrei	vorrebbe	vorremmo	vorrebbero	

Say it simply

1 Imagine you are at the dry cleaner's. You want to know if the item you have brought to be cleaned can be done by the end of the day since you are leaving for Verona early tomorrow morning. You also want to explain that the stain may be red wine.

Think of what you could say in simple Italian, using the words you know. Then write it down and compare it with my suggestion in the **Answers** section.

2 You are at the airport, about to catch your flight home when you realize that you have left some clothes behind in the room of your hotel. You phone the hotel to ask the housekeeper to send the things on to you.

What would you say? Formulate your telephone call and say it. Then write it down and compare it with the one in the **Answers** section.

Spot the keys

Here are two final practice rounds. If you have the recording, close
the book now.

1 This time, the key words are not shown. When you have found
them see if you can get the gist of it. Then look at the answers.

This is what you might ask of a taxi driver:

A quanti minuti è l'aeroporto e quanto costa?

And this could be the reply:

*Dipende da quando va. Normalmente ci vogliono venti minuti,
ma se c'è traffico e se c'è la coda sul ponte ci metterà almeno
trentacinque minuti. Il prezzo lo può vedere sul tachimetro.
Più o meno saranno dai venti ai venticinque euro.*

2 While in the departure lounge of the airport, you overheard
someone raving about something. Identify the key words and guess
where they have been.

*...e anche mio marito dice che delle vacanze così gli piacciono
moltissimo, molto di più di quelle dello scorso anno. La gente
era proprio simpatica e molto più amabile che da noi. L'hotel
era situato proprio in riva al lago; abbiamo fatto delle belle
camminate e il tempo è stato bellissimo. Abbiamo mangiato
benissimo e il prossimo anno ci ritorneremo certamente in...*

Let's speak Italian

🔊 CD2, tr 25

Here's a five-point warm-up: answer these questions using the words in brackets.

1 Ha comprato l'appartamento? (sì, lo)
2 Sa che fanno a Natale? (sì, niente)
3 Quando ha visto suo marito? (ieri)
4 Perché va in Inghilterra? (famiglia, vive, là)
5 Com'è l'Italia? (meravigliosa)

In your last exercise you are going to act as an interpreter again, this time telling your Italian friend what others have said in English. Each time say the whole sentence out loud, translating the English words in brackets.

6 Il mio amico ha detto che... *(the holidays are finished)*.
7 Ha detto anche che... *(we are going to Venice next year)*.
8 Mia moglie vorrebbe sapere... *(when you go to Los Angeles)*.
9 Vorrebbe anche sapere... *(what they said)*.
10 Mio marito dice che... *(he cannot come)*.
11 Angela non può venire perché... *(she works on a ship)*.
12 Il mio amico dice che... *(you are very nice)*.
13 Dice anche che... *(he would like to have your phone number)*.
14 C'è qualcuno che vorrebbe sapere... *(what you did)*.
15 Mia madre dice che... *(she likes the shops)*.
16 Nessuno sa... *(where he has been in America)*.
17 I miei amici non sanno... *(who took the car)*.
18 Qualcuno sa... *(how one can get to Lago Maggiore)*.

Answers

1 Sì, l'ho comprato.
2 Sì, non fanno niente.
3 L'ho visto ieri.
4 Perché la mia famiglia vive là.
5 L'Italia è meravigliosa.
6 ...le vacanze sono finite.
7 ...andiamo a Venezia l'anno prossimo.
8 ...quando va a Los Angeles.
9 ...cosa hanno detto.
10 ...non può venire.
11 ...lavora su una nave.
12 ...Lei è molto simpatico/a.
13 ...vorrebbe avere il suo numero di telefono.
14 ...cosa ha fatto.
15 ...le piacciono i negozi.
16 ...dov'è stato in America.
17 ...chi ha preso l'auto.
18 ...come si può andare al Lago Maggiore.

Let's speak more Italian

🔊 CD2, tr 26

In your own words

This exercise will teach you to express yourself freely. Use only the words you have learned so far.

Tell me in your own words that...

1 next week you have to work
2 you don't like to work; you'd rather have more holidays
3 nobody knows that you are in Milan
4 your mother has the number of your mobile phone
5 your vacation in Tuscany (**Toscana**) was wonderful
6 you did a lot of sightseeing and ate too much
7 your friend Pavarotti works for the Bank of Italy
8 he is going to catch a train to Pisa tomorrow
9 your wife must go to California because her father is ill
10 you would like to go to Miami for Christmas, but by boat

Answers

1 **La settimana prossima devo lavorare.**
2 **Non mi piace lavorare. Vorrei fare più vacanze.**
3 **Nessuno sa che sono a Milano.**
4 **Mia madre ha il numero del mio telefonino.**
5 **La mia vacanza in Toscana era meravigliosa.**
6 **Ho visto molto e ho mangiato troppo.**
7 **Il mio amico Pavarotti lavora alla Banca d'Italia.**
8 **Prende il treno per Pisa domani.**
9 **Mia moglie deve andare in California perché suo padre è malato.**
10 **Vorrei andare a Miami a Natale, ma in nave.**

Let's speak Italian – fast and fluently

◄) CD2, tr 27

Translate each section and check if it is correct, then cover up the answers and say the three or four sentences fast.

Try to say each section in less than 20 seconds.

My company can wait.
Nobody knows where I am.
We call my mother on the mobile.

La mia ditta può aspettare.
Nessuno sa dove sono.
Chiamiamo mia madre sul telefonino.

Next year she would like to go to Venice.
Would you like to come with me?
I don't see anything of interest.

L'anno prossimo lei vorrebbe andare a Venezia.
Vorrebbe venire con me?
Non vedo niente di interessante.

Hello, what are you doing here? What's the matter?
I need to repair my car and my flat. They are very old.
Can you help me, please – with 200 euros?

Salve, cosa fa qui? Che cosa c'è?
Devo riparare l'auto e l'appartamento. Sono molto vecchi.
Può aiutarmi, per favore – con duecento euro?

Now say all the sentences in Italian without stopping and starting.

Test your progress

Thirty verbs have been included in this text. But don't panic – it looks worse than it is. Go for it – you'll do brilliantly!

Translate into Italian:

1 We write many e-mails because we have a new computer.
2 Hello, can I help? Your bag has gone? Where can it be?
3 Who knows the number of his mobile phone? I am sorry, I don't know it.
4 How are you? I am pleased that you do not smoke (any) more.
5 Would you like to see Bologna? It is a big town.
6 I do not like January. There is snow and it is often very cold.
7 There is a kiosk down there. Would you like something to drink?
8 Why have they not phoned? We waited until yesterday.
9 I'll take the book. He says that it is interesting.
10 I believe that the airport is always open, day and night.
11 It is important to know how much the client has bought.
12 Have you seen the English newspaper? I do not like the photo. It is ugly.
13 He said that he has (the) cold. He hopes to come tomorrow.
14 Is an apartment near the centre expensive in Italy?
15 We both have to work. Three boys and two girls cost a lot.
16 I am going at Christmas. I prefer December for my holidays instead of July.
17 We know Marcello very well. Do you like him?
18 Can you give me the dog? He is small but nice. What does he eat?
19 Her mother is here. She does not speak Italian.
20 Don't you know it? The repairs cost 500 euros.
21 I must go to the cashpoint machine. I need money.
22 I am sorry but **Traveller's Italian** is now finished.

Check your answers and then go to the **Progress chart** and work out your final score for the course. You'll be proud of yourself!

Answers

How to score

From a total of 100%

- Subtract 1% for each wrong or missing word.
- Subtract 1% for the wrong form of the verb.
  Example: we have **ho (abbiamo)**.
- Subtract 1% every time you mix up the present and the past tenses.

There are no penalties for:

- wrong use of all those little words, like: **il, la, un, una, il suo, la sua, da il (dal), in il (nel),** etc.
- wrong ending of adjectives, e.g. **un'amica americano**.
- wrong choice of words with similar meaning, e.g.: **a, in, da**.
- wrong or different word order.
- wrong spelling/missing accents/missing apostrophes – as long as you can say the word, e.g.: **bisonyo (bisogno); com'e, comè (com'è)**.

100% MINUS YOUR PENALTIES WILL GIVE YOU YOUR WEEKLY SCORE.

Week 1: Test your progress

1 Buongiorno, siamo Helen e Jane.
2 Sono di Roma, anche Lei?
3 Dove lavora adesso?
4 Sono stato/stata a Milano in ottobre.
5 La mia amica è in Italia per un anno.
6 Andiamo sempre a Pisa in giugno.
7 Ho lavorato alla Fiat in maggio.
8 Che cosa/Cosa fa a Londra?
9 Lavoro in una scuola ma senza soldi.
10 La casa grande a Bologna è per i bambini.
11 Un momento, per favore, dov'è Luigi?
12 La casa ha il telefono? No, purtroppo.
13 Costa molto la Ferrari? Sì, certo, costa troppo.
14 Com'è il lavoro in Italia? Buono?
15 Mario ha un amico/un'amica in una ditta americana.
16 Siamo stati/state a Como per tre giorni.
17 Abbiamo i posti buoni in aereo.
18 Ho sempre le vacanze noiose.
19 Ho bisogno di una bella moglie, una Lamborghini e molti soldi…
20 Telefona adesso con una ditta a Londra.

> Your score: _____ %
> Correct your answers, then read them out loud twice.

Week 2: Test your progress

1 Dove c'è un telefono?
2 Scusi, abbiamo solo la carta di credito.
3 Possiamo mangiare alle sette domani?
4 Ha una tavola abbastanza grande? Siamo in cinque.
5 Le camere piccole non hanno il bagno.
6 Vorremmo mangiare prosciutto e melone.
7 Possiamo andare dalle sei alle sette meno un quarto.
8 Dove possiamo bere qualcosa?
9 Siamo stati al bar dalle nove alle dieci e mezza.
10 Va bene, prendiamo la Fiat per un giorno.
11 Quanto costa la prima colazione? Solo cinque euro.
12 Andiamo a riparare il computer. È rotto.
13 Com'è il latte? Il bambino lo può bere?
14 Dove sono i servizi, a destra o a sinistra?

15 Posso andare a Hollywood – senza mio marito?
16 Un caffè per favore – niente per Lei?
17 Dov'è la Signora Rossi? Forse nel bar?
18 Tre euro e dieci per un tè freddo – è un po' caro...!
19 Sono stato in Toscana in febbraio. Non è male.
20 Ci sono trecento bar qui, uno a cento metri da qui.

Your score: _____ %

Week 3: Test your progress

1 Prima, vorrei passare al Bancomat.
2 In questo negozio le scarpe costano troppo.
3 Ha visto mio marito in farmacia?
4 Siamo stati qui fino alle dieci e un quarto.
5 Abbiamo visto il tennis in Inghilterra, in televisione.
6 Mi dispiace, non abbiamo lo stesso in rosso, nella taglia 44.
7 Questo negozio non è conveniente.
8 Chi ha riparato il mio telefono? Lei?
9 Ecco il grande magazzino. Però non è aperto!
10 Oggi non abbiamo comprato troppo, solo pane e mezzo chilo di burro.
11 Ho mangiato tutto – uova, mele, patate e un pezzo di formaggio.
12 Dobbiamo fare spese. È questo il centro?
13 Ieri sono stato/stata in ditta fino alle nove.
14 I giornali inglesi costano molto in Italia.
15 C'è un autobus? No? Non importa.
16 Era un commesso molto simpatico.
17 Cos'è questo? Qualcosa per noi?
18 Ha comprato la borsa qui vicino o alla UPIM?
19 Era tutto molto caro. Dunque non ho comprato niente.
20 Abbiamo bisogno di tre chili, credo.

Your score: _____ %

Week 4: Test your progress

1 Ha detto che qualcuno ha telefonato? Il Signor Gucci?
2 Vorrei sapere dove sono i ristoranti.
3 È tardi e non c'è. Cosa facciamo stasera?
4 Ecco il menù! Conosce i vini della Toscana?

5 Il Bancomat è su, dietro all'uscita, vicino alla porta.

6 Mercoledì dobbiamo andare dal medico. È un appuntamento importante.

7 Perché dice che è noiosa? Perché la conosco bene.

8 Lo ha visto? Devo andare a Pisa con lui.

9 Il Signor Rossini è il mio cliente. Ha comprato tutto.

10 Vorrei comprare questa cosa. Come si dice in italiano…?

11 La settimana prossima? Mi dispiace. Non è possibile.

12 C'è troppo. Mi aiuti per favore. Grazie mille!

13 Ottanta euro per due giorni? Molto interessante. Sì, naturalmente lo/la prendiamo.

14 Devo comprare tre cose per i miei amici.

15 Dice che ha il raffreddore e che non ha finito il suo lavoro.

16 Possono mangiare solo il minestrone?

17 Mi aiuti per favore. C'è un cane terribile.

18 Nessuno ha visto chi ha mangiato la bistecca.

19 Posso dire qualcosa: il pollo non è male ma il pesce è meglio.

20 Cosa prende? La frutta? Sì certo, è della Toscana.

Your score: _____ %

Week 5: Test your progress

1 È proibito andare al ristorante senza scarpe.

2 Mi piace la sua Lamborghini. Era molto conveniente?

3 Quando sono in viaggio parlo sempre molto italiano.

4 Ho bisogno di sei biglietti. Ci sono posti non fumatori?

5 Speriamo di non avere problemi con il motore.

6 Non mi piace l'Internet. È difficile. Credo di essere troppo vecchio/a.

7 Non capisco. Può parlare più lentamente, per favore?

8 Fa caldo e c'è molta gente qui. Andiamo al lago.

9 Un'ora con lei mi fa venire il mal di testa.

10 C'è un autobus al semaforo. Dove va?

11 La carta di credito è sparita. Dobbiamo telefonare alla polizia.

12 Facciamo così: prima compriamo la Ferrari per me e dopo una T-shirt per Lei.

13 Mi piace quest'auto, però l'altra era meglio.

14 Abbiamo solo un litro di benzina e non c'è un benzinaio fino a Napoli.

15 Mi piace il sole e mi piace la pioggia. Tutti e due mi piacciono.
16 Pronto. Siamo a venti chilometri da Pisa. C'è un meccanico?
17 Scusi, può aiutarmi, per favore? Non conosco Roma. Dov'è la stazione?
18 La strada principale? Non è difficile se prende il metro.
19 Dove sono? Cosa hanno fatto? Non mi piace aspettare.
20 Veniamo dal binario diciassette. Dov'è Mario?

Your score: _____%

Week 6: Test your progress

1 Scriviamo molte e-mail perché abbiamo un computer nuovo.
2 Salve, posso aiutare? La sua borsa è sparita? Dove può essere?
3 Chi sa il numero del suo telefonino? Mi dispiace, non lo so.
4 Come va? Sono contento che non fuma più.
5 Vorrebbe vedere Bologna? È una città grande.
6 Non mi piace gennaio. C'è neve e spesso fa molto freddo.
7 C'è un chiosco laggiù. Desidera qualcosa da bere?
8 Perché non hanno telefonato? Abbiamo aspettato fino a ieri.
9 Prendo il libro. Dice che è interessante.
10 Credo che l'aeroporto è sempre aperto, giorno e notte.
11 È importante sapere quanto ha comprato il cliente.
12 Ha visto il giornale inglese? Non mi piace la foto. È brutta!
13 Ha detto che ha il raffredore. Spera di venire domani.
14 Un appartamento vicino al centro è caro in Italia?
15 Dobbiamo lavorare tutti e due. Tre bambini e due bambine costano molto.
16 Vado a Natale. Preferisco dicembre per le vacanze invece di luglio.
17 Conosciamo Marcello molto bene. Le piace?
18 Può darmi il cane? È piccolo ma simpatico. Cosa mangia?
19 Sua madre è qui. Non parla italiano.
20 Non lo sa? Le riparazioni costano cinquecento euro.
21 Devo passare al Bancomat. Ho bisogno di soldi.
22 Mi dispiace, ma **Traveller's Italian** è finito adesso.

Your score: _____ %

Week 6: Say it simply

1 ...Scusi, ho un grande problema. Forse è vino rosso ma non sono certa. Siamo all'hotel solo fino a domani. Andiamo a Verona alle sette. Lo può fare per stasera per favore?

2 Pronto. Buongiorno, sono Kate Walker. Telefono dall'aeroporto. Sono stata nella camera 22 per tre giorni. Mi dispiace ma ci sono delle mie cose nella camera e come ho detto siamo adesso all'aeroporto e andiamo a Birmingham. Può aiutarmi per favore? L'hotel sa dove sono (vivo) a Birmingham. Molte grazie.

Week 6: Spot the keys

1 It depends when you are going. Normally it takes 20 minutes. But if there is a lot of traffic and there is a queue on the bridge, it takes at least 35 minutes. You can read the price on the meter. It will be between 20 and 25 euros.

2 They had of course been in...*England*!

Italian–English dictionary

In this section you'll find all the **New words** that you have learned, including the 'extras', in alphabetical order.

To make it easy for you to find what you may have forgotten, words are shown exactly as they appear in the **New words** section. For example, if you learned *a lot* you'll find it under 'a'. If you don't remember how to say *I work* you'll find it under 'l'.

The only exceptions to this are the nouns. We've put the article, e.g *the* or **il** following the noun. So you'll find *the car* under 'c' and **il motore** under 'm'.

a to, at
a che ora? at what time?
a destra on the right
a sinistra on the left
abbastanza enough
abbiamo we have
abbiamo mangiato we ate, have eaten
acqua water
adesso now
aeroporto airport
agosto August
aiutare to help
al, alla at, at the
alle cinque at five o'clock
altro/a other
americana American
amica girlfriend
anche also, too
andare to go
andata e ritorno return ticket ('going and returning')
andiamo we go, we are going
anno, un/anni a year/years
aperto open
appartamento apartment, flat

appuntamento appointment
aprile April
arancione orange
aspetta! wait!
aspettare to wait
autobus bus
autostrada motorway

bagno bath
bambino/i child, children
Bancomat cashpoint machine
beh... well...
bellissimo/a very beautiful
bello/a beautiful
bene well, good!
benissimo very good, excellent
benzina petrol
benzinaio petrol station
bere to drink
bianco white
bicchiere, il the glass
biglietto ticket
binario track, platform
birra, birre beer, beers
bistecca steak
blu blue

borsa bag
bottiglia bottle
brutto bad, ugly
buca delle lettere letterbox
buona notte good night
buona sera good evening
buongiorno good day, good morning, hello
buono/a good
burro butter

c'è there is
caffè, il the coffee
calcio football
caldo/a hot
camera room
cameriere, il the waiter
cane, il the dog
carne, la the meat
caro/a expensive, dear
carta di credito credit card
cartina map
cartolina postcard
casa house
cento one hundred
centro centre
certo sure, certain
ci us, we
ci sono there are
ciao hello/goodbye
cinquanta fifty
cinque five
città town, city
cliente, il the client
colori, i the colours
com'è? (come è) how is…?
come how, like, as
come si dice in italiano? how do you say … in Italian?
come va? how are you?
commesso/a sales assistant
comprare to buy
con with
con lui with him
conosciamo we know

conosco I know
contento/a pleased, happy
conto bill
conveniente cheap
cosa desiderano? what would you like?
cosa, una a matter, a thing
cosa? what?
così so
costa it costs
costano they cost
cotoletta alla milanese veal cutlet 'alla milanese'
crede he/she/it believes, you believe
credo I think, believe
che that
che cosa c'è? what's the matter?
che?, che cosa? what?
chi who
chiesa church
chilo kilo
chilometro kilometre
chiosco kiosk

da from, by, at someone's house
da… a from… to/until
da mangiare (something to) eat
dai! come on!
dalle otto… from eight o'clock (lit. from the eight (hours))
dare to give
dato given
davanti a in front of, before
desidera you would like, he/she/it would like
di from, of
dice he/she/it says, you say
dicembre december
diciannove nineteen
diciassette seventeen
diciotto eighteen
dieci ten
dietro a behind
difficile difficult

diritto straight on
ditta firm
dobbiamo we must
doccia shower
dodici twelve
dolori pains
domani tomorrow
domenica Sunday
dopo after, afterwards
doppio/a double
dove? where?
due two
duecento two hundred
dunque therefore, in that case
durante during

e and
è is he/she/it...?, he/she/it is,
   you are
è l'una it is one o'clock
e mezzo half past = and half
e un quarto quarter past = and a
   quarter
ecco here, here is/here are
era was
erano were

fa you do, you make, he/she,
   it does/makes
fa freddo it is cold (used with
   weather)
facciamo we do, make
famiglia family
fanno they do, make
fantastico/a fantastic
fare colazione to have breakfast
fare spese to do (the) shopping
farmacia chemist's, pharmacy
febbraio February
fermata stop
finito finished
fino a until
formaggio cheese
forse perhaps

foto, la/le the photo(s)
francobolli stamps
freddo/a cold
frutta fruit
fuma he/she/it smokes, you smoke
fumare to smoke

gelato ice cream
gennaio January
gente, la the people
giallo yellow
giornale, il the newspaper
giorno, un/giorni a day/days
giovedì Thursday
giugno June
gli the
grammi grams
grande big
grande magazzino department
   store
grazie thank you
grazie mille many (a thousand)
   thanks
grigio grey

ha he/she/it has, you have
ha detto he/she/it has said,
   you said
ho I have
ho bisogno (di) I need
ho comprato I bought, have
   bought
ho lavorato I have worked,
   I worked
ho visto I have seen

i the (plural)
i servizi the toilets
ieri yesterday
il the
il mio, la mia my
il suo his/her (agrees with noun)
importante important
in aereo in the aeroplane

in vacanza on holiday
in viaggio on the move, travelling
Inghilterra England
inglese English
insalata salad
interessante interesting
invece (di) instead (of), on the
   other hand
io I *(only use to emphasize)*

l' the
l'auto (la) the car
l'ospedale the hospital
la the
là there
la Banca d'Italia The Bank of Italy
la mia my
la settimana prossima next week
la sua his/her *(agrees with noun)*
laggiù down there
lago lake
latte, il the milk
lavora you work, he/she/it works
lavoro I work, I am working
lavoro, il the work
le the
Lei you
lentamente slowly
libro book
litro, litri litre, litres
lo, la *(by itself)* it, him, her, you
lo so I know it
lo stesso the same
luglio July
lunedì Monday

ma but
madre, la the mother
maggio May
mai never, ever
mal di testa, il the headache
malato/a sick, ill
male bad
marito husband

marrone brown
martedì Tuesday
marzo March
me, mi me
meccanico mechanic *(at a garage)*
medico doctor
meglio better
meno less/before *(with time)*
meno un quarto quarter to = less a
   quarter
menù, il the menu
meraviglioso/a wonderful
mercoledì Wednesday
mese, il/mesi the month/months
mezzo, mezza half
mi me
mi aiuti, per favore help me, please
mi dispiace I am sorry
mi piace I like
mille one thousand
minuto, un/minuti a minute/minutes
moglie wife
molti soldi a lot of money
molto very, much, a lot
momento, un a moment
motore, il the motor, engine

Natale Christmas
naturalmente of course
nave, la the ship
negozio, negozi shop, shops
nel bar in the bar
nero black
nessuno nobody
neve, la the snow
niente no, nothing, not anything
no no
noi us, we
noioso/a boring
non not
non capisco I don't understand
non fumatori non-smoking
non importa no problem, it doesn't
   matter

non mi piace I do not like it
non si può one cannot
non si può fare one can't do that, that's not on
nostro/a our
notte, la the night
novanta ninety
nove nine
novembre November
numero, numeri number, numbers
nuovo/a new

o or
oggi today
olio oil
ora, un' an hour
ottanta eighty
otto eight
ottobre October

pane, il bread
panino, panini roll, rolls
parlano they speak
parlare to speak
parlo I speak
parrucchiere, il the hairdresser's
passare a/da pass, call on, go to
patate potatoes
patatine, le the chips
pazzo/a crazy
per for
per favore please
perché why, because
però but
pesce, il fish
pezzo piece
piccolo/a small
pieno/a full
pioggia rain
più more
più tardi later
poi then
polizia police

pollo chicken
porta door
possiamo we can
possibile possible
posso I can
posta post office
posti seats, places
prende you take, he/she/it takes
prendere to take
prendiamo we'll take
prendo I take
presto quick, quickly
prima colazione, la the breakfast
primo/a first
problema, il/i problemi the problem/ the problems
proibito forbidden
pronto ready *(and what you say when you answer the phone)*
prosciutto ham
pulito/a clean
può he/she/it/you can
purtroppo unfortunately

qualche some
qualcosa something
qualcuno someone
quando when
quanto/a? how much...?
quaranta forty
quarto quarter
quattordici fourteen
quattro four
questo/a this
qui here
quindici fifteen

raffreddore, un a cold
riparare to repair
riparazioni, le the repairs
ristorante, il the restaurant
rosa pink
rosso red
rotto/a broken

sa he/she/it knows, you know
sabato Saturday
salve hello (*not quite as familiar as* **ciao**)
sapere to know
scarpe, le the shoes
scriviamo we write
scuola school
scusi excuse me
secondo/a second
sedici sixteen
sei six
semaforo traffic light
sempre always
senza without
servizi, i the toilets
sessanta sixty
settanta seventy
sette seven
settembre September
settimana week
sì yes
si può one can
siamo we are
siamo stati we have been, we were
Signor Mr, gentleman
Signora Mrs, woman
simpatico/a nice
sole, il the sun
solo only
sono I am
sono le due it is two o'clock
sono stato/a I have been, I was
sparito/a disappeared
speriamo we hope, let's hope
spesa, la the shopping
spesso often
stasera tonight
stazione, la the (railway) station
strada principale main road
su up, upstairs, *also* on
supermercato supermarket

tabaccaio, il the tobacconist's (*sells stamps*)
taglia size
tavola table
tè, il the tea
telefona she/he telephones
telefonino, il the mobile phone
telefono, il the telephone
televisione, la the TV
tempo weather, time
terribile terrible
tintoria dry cleaner's
torta di mele apple cake (cake of apples)
tre three
tredici thirteen
treno train
trenta thirty
troppo too much
tutti e due both ('all and two')
tutto all

uffa! something you say when you are fed up
ultimo/a last
un po' a little
un pochino a very little
un, una, un' a
undici eleven
uno one
uovo, uova egg, eggs
UPIM, la *well-known Italian chain store*
uscita exit

va bene all right, OK
vado I go, am going
valigia suitcase
vecchio/a old
vedo I see
venerdì Friday
veniamo we come, we are coming
venire to come
venti twenty

103

ventidue twenty-two
ventitré twenty-three
ventuno twenty-one
verde green
verdura vegetables
vicino, vicino a near, near to
vino wine

vive he/she/it lives, you live
vorrebbe he/she/it/you would like
vorrei I would like
vorremmo we would like

zero zero
zucchero sugar

English–Italian dictionary

a **un, una, un'**
a little **un po'**
a lot **molto**
a lot of money **molti soldi**
a very little **un pochino**
after, afterwards **dopo**
airport **aeroporto**
also **anche**
always **sempre**
all **tutto**
all right **va bene**
American **americana**
and **e**
apartment **appartamento**
apple cake (cake of apples) **torta di mele**
appointment **appuntamento**
April **aprile**
at **a**
at five o'clock **alle cinque**
at someone's house **da**
at what time? **a che ora?**
at, at the **al, alla**
August **agosto**

bad **male, brutto**
bag **borsa**
bath **bagno**
beautiful **bello/a**
because **perché**
beer, beers **birra, birre**
before, before *(with time)* **davanti a, meno**
behind **dietro a**
better **meglio**
big **grande**
bill **conto**
black **nero**

blue **blu**
book **libro**
boring **noioso/a**
both ('all and two') **tutti e due**
bottle **bottiglia**
bread **pane, il**
breakfast, the **prima colazione, la**
broken **rotto/a**
brown **marrone**
bus **autobus**
but **ma, però**
butter **burro**
by **da**

call on **passare a/da**
car, the **l'auto (la)**
cashpoint machine **il Bancomat**
centre **centro**
certain **certo**
city **città**
clean **pulito/a**
client, the **cliente, il/la**
coffee, the **caffè, il**
cold **freddo/a**
cold, a **un raffreddore**
colours **i colori**
come on! **dai!**
crazy **pazzo/a**
credit card **carta di credito**
cheap **conveniente**
cheese **formaggio**
chemist's **farmacia**
chicken **pollo**
child, children **bambino/i**
chips, the **patatine, le**
Christmas **Natale**
church **chiesa**

day, days **giorno, giorni**
dear **caro/a**
December **dicembre**
department store **grande magazzino**
difficult **difficile**
disappeared **sparito/a**
doctor **medico**
dog, the **cane, il**
door **porta**
double **doppio/a**
down there **laggiù**
drink **bere**
dry cleaner's **tintoria**
during **durante**

egg, eggs **uovo, uova**
eight **otto**
eighteen **diciotto**
eighty **ottanta**
eleven **undici**
engine, the **motore, il**
England **Inghilterra**
English **inglese**
enough **abbastanza**
ever **mai**
excellent **benissimo**
excuse me **scusi**
exit **uscita**
expensive **caro/a**

family **famiglia**
fantastic **fantastico/a**
February **febbraio**
fifteen **quindici**
fifty **cinquanta**
finished **finito**
firm **ditta**
first **primo/a**
fish **pesce, il**
five **cinque**
flat **appartamento**
football **calcio**
for **per**
forbidden **proibito**
forty **quaranta**

fourteen **quattordici**
Friday **venerdì**
from **di, da**
from... to/until **da... a**
from eight o'clock (*lit.* from the eight
    (hours)) **dalle otto...**
fruit **frutta**
full **pieno/a**

gentleman **signor(e)**
girlfriend **amica**
give **dare**
given **dato**
glass, the **bicchiere, il**
go to **passare a/da**
good **buono/a, bene**
good day **buongiorno**
good evening **buona sera**
good morning **buongiorno**
good night **buona notte**
goodbye **ciao**
grams **grammi**
green **verde**
grey **grigio**

hairdresser's, the **parrucchiere, il**
half **mezzo, mezza**
half past = and half **e mezzo**
ham **prosciutto**
happy **contento/a**
he/she/it believes, you believe
    crede
he/she/it/you can **può**
he/she/it has, you have **ha**
he/she/it has said, you said **ha detto**
he/she/it is **è**
he/she/it knows, you know **sa**
he/she/it lives, you live **vive**
he/she/it makes, you make **fa**
he/she/it says, you say **dice**
he/she/it smokes, you smoke **fuma**
he/she telephones **telefona**
he/she/it/you would like **vorrebbe**
headache, the **mal di testa, il**
help me, please **mi aiuti, per favore**
hello **buongiorno, ciao**

four **quattro**

hello *(not quite as familiar as ciao)* **salve**
her *(agrees with noun)* **la sua**
her **lo, la** *(by itself)*
here, here is/here are **qui, ecco**
him **lo, la** *(by itself)*
his/her (agrees with noun) **il suo**
hospital, the **l'ospedale**
hot **caldo/a**
hour, an **un'ora**
house **casa**
how **come**
how are you? **come va?**
how do you say … in Italian? **come si dice in italiano?**
how is…? **com'è? (come è)**
how much…? **quanto/a?**
husband **marito**

I *(only use to emphasize)* **io**
I am **sono**
I am sorry **mi dispiace**
I believe **credo**
I bought, have bought **ho comprato**
I can **posso**
I do not like it **non mi piace**
I don't understand **non capisco**
I go, am going **vado**
I have **ho**
I have been **sono stato/a**
I have seen **ho visto**
I have worked, I worked **ho lavorato**
I know **conosco**
I know it **lo so**
I like **mi piace**
I need **ho bisogno (di)**
I see **vedo**
I speak **parlo**
I take **prendo**
I think **credo**
I was **sono stato/a**
I work, I am working **lavoro**
I would like **vorrei**
ice cream **gelato**
ill **malato/a**
important **importante**

in front of **davanti a**
in that case **dunque**
in the aeroplane **in aereo**
in the bar **nel bar**
instead (of) **invece (di)**
interesting **interessante**
is he/she/it…? **è?**
it costs **costa**
it doesn't matter **non importa**
it is cold *(used with weather)* **fa freddo**
it is one o'clock **è l'una**
it is two o'clock **sono le due**
it, him, her, you **lo, la** *(by itself)*

January **gennaio**
July **luglio**
June **giugno**

kilo **chilo**
kilometre **chilometro**
kiosk **chiosco**

lake **lago**
last **ultimo/a**
later **più tardi**
less **meno**
let's hope **speriamo**
letterbox **buca delle lettere**
like **come**
litre, litres **litro, litri**

main road **strada principale**
many (a thousand) thanks **grazie mille**
map **cartina**
March **marzo**
matter, a **cosa, una**
May **maggio**
me **me, mi**
meat, the **carne, la**
mechanic *(at a garage)* **meccanico**
menu, the **menù, il**
milk, the **latte, il**
minute, minutes **minuto, minuti**
mobile phone, the **telefonino, il**

107

momento **moment**
Monday **lunedì**
months, the **i mesi**
more **più**
mother, the **madre, la**
motor, the **motore, il**
motorway **autostrada**
Mr **Signor**
Mrs **Signora**
much **molto**
my **il mio, la mia**

near **vicino**
near to **vicino a**
never **mai**
new **nuovo/a**
newspaper, the **giornale, il**
next week **la settimana prossima**
nice **simpatico/a**
night, the **notte, la**
nine **nove**
nineteen **diciannove**
ninety **novanta**
no **no, niente**
no problem **non importa**
nobody **nessuno**
non-smoking **non fumatori**
not **non**
not anything **niente**
nothing **niente**
November **novembre**
now **adesso**
numbers **i numeri**

October **ottobre**
of **di**
of course **naturalmente**
often **spesso**
oil **olio**
OK **va bene**
old **vecchio/a**
on **su**
on holiday **in vacanza**
on the left **a sinistra**
on the move **in viaggio**

on the other hand **invece (di)**
on the right **a destra**
one **uno**
one can **si può**
one can't do that **non si può fare**
one cannot **non si può**
one hundred **cento**
one thousand **mille**
only **solo**
open **aperto**
or **o**
orange **arancione**
other **altro/a**
our **nostro/a**

pains **dolori**
pass **passare a/da**
people, the **gente, la**
perhaps **forse**
petrol **benzina**
petrol station **benzinaio**
pharmacy **farmacia**
photo(s), the **la/le foto**
piece **pezzo**
pink **rosa**
places **posti**
platform **binario**
please **per favore**
pleased **contento/a**
police **polizia**
possible **possibile**
post office **posta**
postcard **cartolina**
potatoes **patate**
problems, the **i problemi**

quarter **quarto**
quarter past = and a quarter
   e un quarto
quarter to = less a quarter **meno un
   quarto**
quick, quickly **presto**

(railway) station, the **stazione, la**
rain **pioggia**

ready (and what you say when you answer the phone) **pronto**
red **rosso**
repairs, the **riparazioni, le**
restaurant, the **ristorante, il**
return ticket ('going and returning') **andata e ritorno**
roll, rolls **panino, panini**
room **camera**

salad **insalata**
sales assistant **commesso/a**
same, the **lo stesso**
Saturday **sabato**
school **scuola**
seats **posti**
second **secondo/a**
September **settembre**
seven **sette**
seventeen **diciassette**
seventy **settanta**
she/he telephones **telefona**
ship, the **nave, la**
shoes, the **scarpe, le**
shop, shops **negozio, negozi**
shopping, the **spesa, la**
shower **doccia**
sick **malato/a**
six **sei**
sixteen **sedici**
sixty **sessanta**
size **taglia**
slowly **lentamente**
small **piccolo/a**
snow, the **neve, la**
so **così**
some **qualche**
someone **qualcuno**
something **qualcosa**
something to eat **qualcosa da mangiare**
something you say when you are fed up **uffa!**
stamps **francobolli**
steak **bistecca**

stop **fermata**
straight on **diritto**
sugar **zucchero**
suitcase **valigia**
sun, the **sole, il**
Sunday **domenica**
supermarket **supermercato**
sure **certo**

table **tavola**
tea, the **tè, il**
telephone, the **telefono, il**
ten **dieci**
terrible **terribile**
thank you **grazie**
that **che**
that's not on **non si può fare**
the **gli, i, il, l', la, le**
The Bank of Italy **la Banca d'Italia**
then **poi**
there **là**
there are **ci sono**
there is **c'è**
therefore **dunque**
they cost **costano**
they do **fanno**
they make **fanno**
they speak **parlano**
thing, a **cosa, una**
thirteen **tredici**
thirty **trenta**
this **questo/a**
three **tre**
Thursday **giovedì**
ticket **biglietto**
time **il tempo**
to **a**
to buy **comprare**
to come **venire**
to do (the) shopping **fare spese**
to go **andare**
to have breakfast **fare colazione**
to help **aiutare**
to know **sapere**
to repair **riparare**

to smoke **fumare**
to speak **parlare**
to take **prendere**
to wait **aspettare**
tobacconist's *(sells stamps)*, the
   tabaccaio, il
today **oggi**
toilets, the **i servizi**
tomorrow **domani**
tonight **stasera**
too **anche**
too much **troppo**
town **città**
track **binario**
traffic light **semaforo**
train **treno**
travelling **in viaggio**
Tuesday **martedì**
TV, the **televisione, la**
twelve **dodici**
twenty **venti**
twenty-one **ventuno**
twenty-three **ventitré**
twenty-two **ventidue**
two **due**
two hundred **duecento**

ugly **brutto**
unfortunately **purtroppo**
until **fino a**
up **su**
upstairs **su**
us **ci, noi**

veal cutlet 'alla milanese'
   cotoletta alla milanese
vegetables **verdura**
very **molto**
very beautiful **bellissimo/a**
very good **benissimo**

wait! **aspetta!**
waiter, the **cameriere, il**
was **era**
water **acqua**

we **ci, noi**
we are **siamo**
we ate, have eaten **abbiamo**
   mangiato
we can **possiamo**
we come, we are coming **veniamo**
we do, make **facciamo**
we go, we are going **andiamo**
we have **abbiamo**
we have been **siamo stati**
we hope **speriamo**
we know **conosciamo**
we must **dobbiamo**
we were **siamo stati**
we would like **vorremmo**
we write **scriviamo**
we'll take **prendiamo**
weather *(also time)* **tempo**
Wednesday **mercoledì**
week **settimana**
well, well… **bene, beh…**
well-known Italian chain store
   UPIM, la
were **erano**
what would you like? **cosa**
   desiderano?
what? **che?, che cosa? cosa?**
what's the matter? **che cosa c'è?**
when **quando**
where? **dove?**
white **bianco**
who **chi**
why **perché**
wife **moglie**
wine **vino**
with **con**
with him **con lui**
without **senza**
woman **signora**
wonderful **meraviglioso/a**
work, the **lavoro, il**

year, years **anno, anni**
yellow **giallo**
yes **sì**

yesterday **ieri**
you **Lei, la (by itself)**
you are **è**
you do/do you do? **fa**
you take, he/she/it takes **prende**

you work, he/she/it works **lavora**
you would like, he/she/it would like
   desidera

zero **zero**

How to use the flash cards

Learning words and sentences can be tedious but with flash cards it's quick and good fun.

This is what you do

When the **Day-by-day guide** tells you to use the cards cut them out, photocopy them or copy them on to card. There are 22 **Flash words** and 10 **Flash sentences** for each week. Each card has a little number on it telling you to which week it belongs. So you won't cut out too many cards at a time or muddle them up later on.

First try to learn the words and sentences by looking at both sides. Then, when you have a rough idea, start testing yourself – that's the fun bit. Look at the English, say the Italian, and then check. Make 'correct', 'wrong' and 'don't know' piles. When all cards are used up, start again with the 'wrong' pile and try to whittle it down until you get all of them right. You can also play it 'backwards' by starting with the Italian face-up.

Take the cards with you on the bus, the train, to the hairdresser's or the dentist's. Do a quik 'turn and learn' whenever you have a bit of spare time.

The 22 **Flash words** of each lesson are there to start you off. Convert the rest of the **New words** to **Flash cards**, too. It's well worth it!

Flash cards for fast learning:
Don't lose them – use them!

---

1 **abbiamo**	1 **siamo**
1 **purtroppo**	1 **andiamo**
1 **vado**	1 **sono stato/ sono stata**
1 **il mio, la mia**	1 **ditta**
1 **che?, che cosa?, cosa?**	1 **fa**
1 **ho lavorato**	1 **adesso**

1 **we are**	1 **we have**
1 **we go, let's go**	1 **unfortunately**
1 **I was, I have been**	1 **I go**
1 **company, firm**	1 **my**
1 **you do, he/she/it does**	1 **what?**
1 **now**	1 **I worked, I have worked**

Cut out and use ✂

siamo stati/e 1	**come** 1
com'è? 1	**ho bisogno(di)** 1
sempre 1	**senza** 1
dove 1	**con** 1
i soldi 1	**la casa** 1
la camera 2	**forse** 2

how 1	we were, we have been 1
I need 1	how is? 1
without 1	always 1
with 1	where 1
the house 1	the money 1
perhaps 2	the room 2

Cut out and use ✂

2	2
abbastanza	**un po'**
2	2
male	**quanto**
2	2
va bene	**la prima colazione**
2	2
c'è	**diritto**
2	2
qualcosa	**solo**
2	2
il conto	**troppo**

2	2
a little	**enough**
2	2
how much	**bad**
2	2
breakfast	**all right, OK**
2	2
straight on	**there is**
2	2
only	**something**
2	2
too, too much	**the bill**

Cut out and use

2 **poi**	2 **qui**
2 **a sinistra**	2 **a destra**
2 **meno**	2 **il marito**
2 **può**	2 **i servizi**
3 **oggi**	3 **dobbiamo**
3 **tutto**	3 **dopo**

2 **here**	2 **then**
2 **(on the) right**	2 **(on the) left**
2 **the husband**	2 **less**
2 **the toilets**	2 **you can, he/she/it can**
3 **we must**	3 **today**
3 **after, afterwards**	3 **all**

Cut out and use ✂

3	3
fino a	**quando**
3	3
più tardi	**pezzo**
3	3
ieri	**vicino**
3	3
lo stesso	**questo**
3	3
francobolli	**comprare**
3	3
credo	**ho comprato**

3	3
when	**until**
3	3
piece	**later**
3	3
near	**yesterday**
3	3
this	**the same**
3	3
to buy	**stamps**
3	3
I have bought	**I believe**

Cut out and use ✂

3 **chi**	3 **aperto/a**
3 **la farmacia**	3 **niente**
3 **vorrei**	3 **non importa**
4 **qualcuno**	4 **perché?**
4 **un appuntamento**	4 **benissimo!**
4 **l'uscita**	4 **davanti a**

Cut out and use

3 **open**	3 **who**
3 **nothing**	3 **the pharmacy**
3 **it doesn't matter**	3 **I would like**
4 **why,** *also:* **because**	4 **someone**
4 **excellent!**	4 **an appointment**
4 **in front of**	4 **the exit**

Cut out and use ✂

stasera 4	**che** 4
dietro a 4	**su** 4
nessuno 4	**meglio** 4
certo 4	**posso** 4
come 4	**una cosa** 4
conosco 4	**conosco** 4

4	4
that, *also:* what?	tonight
on	behind
better	nobody
I can	sure, certain
a thing, matter	like, as *also:* how?
a glass	I know

Cut out and use ✂

4	4
con lui	**dice**

4	4
un cane	**dolori**

5	5
biglietto	**aspettare**

5	5
presto	**fermata**

5	5
altro/a	**sparito/a**

5	5
semaforo	**caldo/a**

4	4
he/she says	**with him**
4	4
pains	**a dog**
5	5
to wait	**ticket**
5	5
stop	**quick, quickly**
5	5
gone, disappeared	**other**
5	5
warm, hot	**traffic light**

Cut out and use ✂

5	5
pioggia	**benzina**

5	5
dare/dato	**...mi piace**

5	5
più	**strada principale**

5	5
tutti e due	**vecchio/a**

5	5
venire	**contento/a**

5	5
il problema	**capisco**

Cut out and use ✂

5	5
petrol	**rain**
5	5
I like…	**to give/given**
5	5
main road	**more**
5	5
old	**both**
5	5
pleased, happy	**to come**
5	5
I understand	**the problem**

Cut out and use ✂

5	5
proibito	**pieno/a**

5	5
Salve!	**città**

6	6
aeroporto	**a Natale**

6	6
libro	**appartamento**

6	6
le riparazioni	**laggiù**

6	6
la neve	**lo so**

5 **full**	5 **forbidden**
5 **town**	5 **Hello!**
6 **at Christmas**	6 **airport**
6 **apartment, flat**	6 **book**
6 **down there**	6 **the repairs**
6 **I know it**	6 **the snow**

Cut out and use ✂

6	6
mai	**vedo**
conosciamo	**fanno**
invece (di)	**meraviglioso/a**
spesso	**la nave**
la madre	**ha detto**
l'aeroporto	**la famiglia**

Cut out and use ✂

6	6
I see	**never, ever**

6	6
they do	**we know**

6	6
wonderful	**instead (of)**

6	6
the ship	**often**

6	6
he/she said	**the mother**

6	6
the family	**the airport**

Cut out and use

Buongiorno, sono... 1

un momento per favore... 1

Andiamo a Firenze. 1

Venezia è molto bella. 1

Lavoro a Londra. 1

per la mia ditta 1

Ho bisogno di molti soldi. 1

Adesso siamo in vacanza. 1

Abbiamo una casa. 1

Sono stato/stata in Italia. 1

Good morning, I am... [1]

one moment, please... [1]

We go/Let's go to Florence. [1]

Venice is very beautiful. [1]

I work in London. [1]

for my company [1]

I need a lot of money. [1]

We are on holiday now. [1]

We have a house. [1]

I was/have been in Italy. [1]

Cut out and use ✂

Ha una camera?

2

Dov'è la camera?

2

Quanto costa?

2

a che ora

2

Vorremmo andare a Roma.

2

alle otto e mezza

2

È troppo caro.

2

C'è un bar qui?

2

qualcosa da mangiare

2

il conto per favore

2

Cut out and use ✂

Do you have a room? 2

Where is the room? 2

How much does it cost? 2

at what time 2

We would like to go to Rome. 2

at half past eight 2

It is too expensive. 2

Is there a bar here? 2

something to eat 2

the bill, please 2

Cut out and use

Mi dispiace. 3

Dobbiamo andare. 3

Vorrei fare spese. 3

Devo passare al Bancomat. 3

fino a quando 3

C'è un negozio? 3

Non importa. 3

Ho comprato troppo. 3

È molto simpatico. 3

vicino alla posta 3

Cut out and use

I am sorry. 3

We must go. 3

I want to go shopping. 3

I must go to the cashpoint machine. 3

until when 3

Is there a shop? 3

It doesn't matter. 3

I have bought too much. 3

He is very nice. 3

near the post office 3

Cut out and use

C'è qualcuno.

4

Non ha detto.

4

la settimana prossima

4

davanti alla porta

4

dietro alla chiesa

4

Non abbiamo tempo.

4

Andiamo a mangiare.

4

Vado con lui.

4

Mi aiuti per favore.

4

Come si dice in italiano…?

4

There is someone. 4

He did not say. 4

next week 4

in front of the door 4

behind the church 4

We don't have time. 4

We are going to eat. 4

I('ll) go with him. 4

Help me, please. 4

How do you say in Italian…? 4

Cut out and use

andata e ritorno 5

Mi dispiace, non capisco. 5

Può parlare più lentamente? 5

A che ora c'è un treno? 5

Sono molto contento. 5

Mi piace la Fiat. 5

Mi piace, perché è nuova. 5

Mi piacciono tutti e due. 5

Il vino non mi piace. 5

Si può fumare qui? 5

Cut out and use

return (ticket) 5

I am sorry, I don't understand? 5

Can you speak more slowly? 5

At what time is there a train? 5

I am very happy. 5

I like the Fiat. 5

I like it because it is new. 5

I like both. 5

I don't like wine. 5

Can one smoke here? 5

Cut out and use ✂

Nessuno lo sa. 6

Non lo so. 6

Che cosa c'è? 6

Cosa ha detto? 6

Cosa fanno? 6

Come va? 6

Non vedo… 6

Non c'è niente. 6

Non sono mai stato. 6

Andiamo da un amico. 6

Cut out and use

Nobody knows it.

6

I don't know it.

6

What is it?/What is there?

6

What did he say?

6

What are they doing?

6

How are you?

6

I do not see...

6

There is nothing.

6

I have never been.

6

We are going to a friend's.

6

Cut out and use

This is to certify
that

....

has successfully completed
a six-week course of

Traveller's Italian
with

....

results

Date ....

Author Elizabeth Smith

Praise for Elisabeth Smith

'A language lifeline ... fun, fast and easy.'
(*The Independent*)

'The simple scripts and audio make it crystal clear ... I'm delighted with my progress.'
(*Greece* magazine)

'Its narration is laid-back and encouraging and the method is straightforward. (4-star review)'
(*Time Out*)

'The elements are simple and very straightforward ... strong encouragement ... plenty of opportunity for spoken practice. This course worked very well for me.'
(*Professional Manager* magazine)

'We think it is wonderful.'
(Tom and Maureen Peil, Preston)

'I loved the sense of humour ... Each week I did the final test with bated breath wondering if this time the little bar chart [...] would take a nose dive – but it didn't.'
(Lesly Hopkins, Twickenham)

'This isn't just a package that asks you remember the names for things in a different language this is a package that teaches ... Highly recommended.'
(Maximus)

'It really is an effective way to learn.'
(Mr R. Ellor)

'A solid product offering excellent value for money ... a great place to start.'
(A. M. Boughey)

'One of the best courses around to get you that little bit further than the basics.'
(Johannsen Krister)

more...

'The words are very clearly spoken and the form of presentation witty and lively to keep your interest, and clever choice of subject matter also keep learning interesting and aid memory. This is a very strong language course and I recommend it.'
(vh1967)

'The Elisabeth Smith courses are a superb resource for the learner who needs to be able to speak the language in a short period of time and with a good degree of understanding.'
(Will Boyce)

'I was surprised at what I'd achieved after this course and recommend it.'

'This is an absolute must have … You'll be so glad you bought it!'
(Elodie)

Now join me on:

Facebook at www.facebook.com/elisabethsmithlanguages

Twitter at www.twitter.com/LanguagesESmith